I'm so thankful for the many incredible relationships I've had the privilege of building over the years. I am honored to have numerous friends and mentors who, had I asked, would have been willing to endorse this book. But after much prayer and consideration, I have decided to request only two endorsements for this book. The first endorsement is that of the Holy Spirit. I ask Him to endorse this book by causing it to speak with clarity, power, and revelation to every individual who reads it. I ask Him to endorse it by using the words on these pages to heal hearts, calm spirits, and empower readers to gain authority over the spirit of Jezebel that may have afflicted them. Second, I ask for your endorsement. If this book ministers to you, I ask you to endorse it by applying this revelation to gain freedom and deliverance in your own life. Then I ask you to share it with any-one with whom you come into contact that the spirit of Jezebel has afflicted.

Jezebel

The Witch Is Back

Landon Schott

Jezebel: The Witch Is Back
© 2013 Landon Schott

Famous Publishing
Spokane, WA

ISBN: 978-1-940243-03-0

Library of Congress Control Number: 2013946463

ACKNOWLEDGMENTS

I would like to thank God for the opportunity to write this book to help a new generation of believers and ministers recognize and confront the spirit of Jezebel. This spirit is only defeated through the discernment of the Spirit of God and the powerful blood of Jesus.

I want to thank my incredible wife, Heather Lynn Schott, for introducing the revelation of Jezebel to me. Thank you for standing by me and loving me. I would not be in ministry today if it had not been for you. I honor you. I love you, darling!

I'm eternally grateful to John Paul Jackson for the investment he has made into my life and this book. Thank you for your love, support, and continual example of humility. I'm exceptionally honored that you would write such an insightful foreword as well as the prayers in chapter 3 and 4. Special thanks to Chris Gilkey, Eida Diego, Ron Kerr, Kari Kerr, and Dr. Alan Bullock for your prayers, contributions, and insights.

I would like to give special thanks to Jim Kochenburger for editing this book, S.C. for proofreading and Evan Leake, who created the exceptional cover design. It has been a blessing working with all of you.

TABLE OF CONTENTS

FOREWORD

It was an age of apostasy. A nation God called to be His own had turned against Him. It had exchanged its worship of God for the idols of a people it had once conquered in His name. The king who ruled Israel was the son of a man who gained his kingship through assassination. His name, Ahab, was to become synonymous with evil.

Behind the corruption of Ahab's throne was a woman—Jezebel. Hoping to expand her power by marrying Ahab, she ushered in one of the darkest, most destructive eras in Israel's history. Her impetus was fanatical devotion to two false gods; Baal, the male deity of power and sexuality, and Ashtoreth, the female goddess of fertility, love, and war. Baal and Ashtoreth worship rituals involved depraved, licentious sexual practices and abominations which appealed to the bestial, material elements in human nature. (The Baal idol even resembled the male sexual organ and the altar to Ashtoreth resembled the female sexual organ.) More than 450 prophets of Baal and 400 prophetesses of Ashtoreth served Jezebel's depraved, carnal desires, often sacrificing human lives to appease these pagan deities.

God raised up the prophet Elijah to challenge Ahab's apostasy and destroy the prophets of Baal on Mt. Carmel. As a countermove, Satan raised up his messenger to silence God's prophetic voice: Ahab's wife, Queen Jezebel.

We, too are living in an age of impending apostasy. Our society is quickly turning its back on God. Far too often we hear reports of how sin has infected the Body of Christ and its leaders. Yet amidst the crescendo of decadence and depravity in our day, God is raising up a prophetic generation. This generation will carry the spirit of Elijah. It will be anointed to perform miraculous signs and wonders and will accomplish great exploits for the Kingdom of God.

Just as he has done from the beginning, Satan is raising up fierce opposition to this prophetic generation. The enemy has always sought to silence God's prophetic voices and abort intercessory prayer. Once again, its name is Jezebel—a diabolical spiritual force that seeks to deceive, defile, and destroy God's authorities.

Jezebel, the destroyer of leaders to whom she promised success, was as intimidating in the Old Testament as she was in the New Testament. Of all the villains named in the Bible, none knew how to use intimidation, manipulation, deceit, and flattery (mixed with feigned meekness) more artfully than Jezebel to get what they wanted.

The only certainty you have in dealing with this spirit is this: "Nothing is as it seems." This spirit is as devious as they come and can work through both males and females, which makes facing it even more complicated. It lives vicariously on the influence of others, all the while making leaders think it is all about them.

An illustration of how the Jezebel spirit works can be easily seen in how a virus enters a computer. When a computer is attacked by a virus, its antivirus program will indicate a malicious program is attempting to cause it to function contrary to its operating system. The antivirus program will then tell the computer how to recognize the virus and trash it. Depending on the degree of damage caused by the virus, to operate effectively, the computer may need reprogramming.

In the Kingdom, when an alien force—a Jezebel power—is downloaded into a church, its goal is to disable and destroy individuals, ministries—even the church as a whole. It will succeed unless God's remedy—a divine antivirus program—is applied. If pastors are unable to detect or prevent this spirit's operation, their spouses, children, or church members may fall prey to its devious ploys.

While it is true that from time to time most people behave in a controlling manner to some extent, with Jezebel, these tendencies become a lifestyle. There are no clear-cut indicators when a person steps over the line, but a line is crossed nonetheless. It does not happen in the blink of an eye. Opening one's soul to operate in a Jezebel spirit is a process that expands and deepens much as the limbs and roots of a tree. The longer one operates in a controlling and manipulative manner without repenting, the stronger and deeper the spirit grows. Eventually, it becomes one's primary way of relating to others. If left unaddressed, it will silently gain control and stealthily make inroads into the authority structure of the church.

Although the illustrations of Jezebel in Scripture are female-oriented, this demonic power does not simply infect women. Men have operated in this spirit as well. When this occurs, they are left weakened and emasculated by the demonic presence. However, it is difficult for men to operate under the influence of this spirit for very long because it needs an Ahab spirit to keep it alive.

A pastor or leader can choose to be an Ahab and empower a Jezebel spirit, an Elijah and identify it (only to run from it), or a Jehu and remove it. Leaders can choose the part they play, but they cannot ignore this spirit. Jezebel won't let them.

Landon Schott has done a remarkable job of detailing how to recognize the Jezebel spirit. He has done so using language the upcoming prophetic generation will readily recognize. With uncommon insight, Landon delineates how to deal with and overcome this spirit, enduing readers with courage to do so. I am honored Landon asked me to write this foreword.

May king-like champions arise and may the works of the evil one be destroyed.

John Paul Jackson
Founder
Streams Ministries International

INTRODUCTION

It was one of the darkest moments of my life. I remember leaning against the wall of our little two-bedroom apartment, slowly sliding down until finally, I slumped down onto the floor. Alarmed, my wife asked me what was wrong and other questions, but I couldn't answer her. I felt as if someone had reached down my throat and ripped the breath straight out of my lungs. I felt as if I were in a demonic haze. I couldn't process my thoughts. I tried to speak but nothing came out. My wife began to shout louder: "Babe, what's wrong? Answer me!" Tears welled up in her eyes. I didn't answer her. I had no answers.

I was under heavy spiritual oppression, and it had immersed me in confusion and bewilderment. This demonic attack made me feel as if I were losing my mind! I remember being convinced God didn't want to use me anymore, that I wasn't valuable to Him. Worst of all, I had lost all spiritual vision, all hope. It was the darkest moment of my life.

I'll never forget my wife walking over to me at just that moment, laying her hands on my head, and boldly praying over me. She pleaded the blood of Jesus and rebuked the spirit of Jezebel. After a few moments, the oppression lifted.

Many Christians have shared similar experiences with demonic attacks. Some are too embarrassed to admit it, while others are unaware of what is really going on. But they have suffered the fierce internal struggle of at one moment feeling absolutely confident in what God has called them to do, only in the next moment to feel they don't know up from down, spiritually. They've lived through the torment of a fear of failure so constant and unrelenting that they are driven to believe, almost on a weekly basis, that they should give up on their faith or quit the ministry. They know what it feels like to wonder if they are going crazy.

As the spirit of Jezebel works its witchcraft, some people are burdened so heavily by anxiety that they can feel it physically, as if someone is sitting on their chest, even as they stand. It is so strong that they don't even want to be awake anymore. Sometimes, they lose even their will to live. More than anything, this spirit of Jezebel can cause even the most dedicated Christians to want to abort the call of God on their lives—to just *give up and quit!* All these are the effects of the spirit of Jezebel...of witchcraft.

Many Christians have determined that witchcraft is make-believe, or only believed in by extremists. We hear reports of witchcraft from the mission field, but don't believe it can affect our lives. In reality, Christians unknowingly experience witchcraft on a regular basis.

Witchcraft is rooted in rebellion (1 Samuel 15:23); its central focus is controlling the will of others through fear, manipulation, intimidation, and domination. When witchcraft attacks, many people experience anxiety, confusion, intimidation, continual unexplained sickness, chronic pain, depression, and fatigue. All these symptoms and more are physical, spiritual, and psychological effects of what we refer to as the spirit of Jezebel. We need to recognize witchcraft in its true form, not as the Hollywood variety, with its dramatized voodoo dolls, or ladies flying on broomsticks and casting spells. Witchcraft is very real, and it is really destroying the lives of God's servants.

It is important to understand that despite the many references in this book to the biblical character of Jezebel and the modern-day "Jezebels" who cause division or trouble in the church, when we talk about the spirit of Jezebel, we are not talking about single individuals. Historically, when we talk about the spirit of Jezebel, we are referring to an eccentric individual or weird lady who is divisive or causes trouble in the church. The spirit of Jezebel is so much more than this.

It is also important to understand that the spirit of Jezebel is not gender-specific, though it will be referred to as "she" or "her" throughout this book. Many men as well as women have been influenced by this spirit without realizing it. Due to the emasculation of men in our society today, more and more of them are being influenced by the spirit of Jezebel.

Jezebel was a heathen queen who introduced God's people to the worship of Baal through compromise, seduction, fear, and murder. She stopped at nothing to get what she wanted. She tormented God's people and inflicted catastrophic fear in the hearts of even God's most renowned prophets. Remember Elijah the prophet boldly confronted 450 prophets of Baal on Mt. Carmel and God answered him with fire. Even after all that, after an encounter with Jezebel, Elijah ran in fear and asked God to take his life. Jezebel rose up to silence the prophetic Word of God. Anytime the Spirit of God moves and a prophetic voice is raised or ministry arises, a spirit of Jezebel will always mobilize to destroy it, warring against it.

The spirit of Jezebel is a form of Antichrist spirit. In 1 John 2:18 (NKJV), we read, "Little children, it is the last hour; and as you have heard that the Antichrist is coming, even now many antichrists have come, by which we know that it is the last hour." The Jezebel spirit is a religious, political, sensual, seductive, manipulative, and controlling spirit that desires to rule over everything in our lives, families, workplaces, or ministries, particularly in this *last hour*. Throughout this book, we will expose the spirit of Jezebel, the spirit behind it, the person, and how countless individuals—male and female—have been influenced by this spirit.

We are living in the days of Elijah, the days the prophet Joel spoke of: God is pouring out His Spirit on His people again (Joel 2:28). God is pouring out His Spirit all over the world. God's Church is rising up and taking its rightful place in the world. Across the globe, ministries are exploding as millions are coming to know Jesus. The gifts of the Spirit are manifesting through teenagers. God's Spirit is moving mightily!

But when God's Spirit is moving, know that the spirit of Jezebel is on her way to try to stop it!

As God has begun to pour out His Spirit as He promised, the spirit of Jezebel has made her way back into culture, media, politics, and the Church. It is back in full force, working to destroy prophetic voices and those who have given their lives to make Jesus famous.

I've entitled this book, *Jezebel: The Witch Is Back*. The witch is back in a sexually charged Hollywood. Movies have spread her perversions and sexuality across the world to billions of people. Universities are filled with secularist philosophers and professors who hate God and love to try to disprove Him. We have become a pro-choice society that has traded righteousness for a woman's right to choose self-worship. Pornography has made its way past magazines and onto phones. The pornography industry grosses more yearly revenue than every major sport *combined!*[1]

Homosexuality has driven its agenda into the heart of society and we are watching God's institution of marriage trampled at the feet of "tolerance and equality." Jezebel is back on the scene! In Malachi 4:5-6 (NLT), we read: "See, I will send the prophet Elijah to you before that great and dreadful day of the LORD comes. His preaching will turn the hearts of fathers to their children, and the hearts of children to their fathers."

This book will describe in great detail the characteristics and strategy the spirit of Jezebel has used historically to war against God's people. It will show how this spirit infiltrates churches, pastors, families, and friends, and the ability it has to destroy even the closest, most important relationships in your life. It will reveal how this spirit has made its way into the secular media, the entertainment industry, and even your workplace. We will address how Jezebel navigates her deception and the spirits with which she aligns herself. Most importantly, this book will teach you how to expose, confront, and wage spiritual war against it and follow the example of Jesus to become victorious over the Jezebel spirit.

Before you begin reading, I want to give you a friendly but serious warning: Jezebel doesn't like to be talked about. She doesn't like to be exposed. She wants to remain hidden, with full control over your life, mind, and soul. As you begin to expose this spirit and how it operates through people, it will stop at nothing to keep you bound in fear, confusion, and torment.

The stories in this book are drawn from actual situations in churches and other ministry organizations. As you read, you will learn the spirit of Jezebel targets prophetic, Spirit-led, soul-winning ministries, even through pastors and spiritual leaders. It should be understood that this in *no way* gives anyone license to rebel against pastors or church leaders they encounter. Those who find themselves unable to trust, obey, or submit to church leaders would be wise to understand that the spirit of Jezebel has already begun to influence them. I encourage you, prayerfully and humbly ask the Holy Spirit to speak to you, give you a submissive heart, and minister to you as you continue reading.

As you share the truth about the spirit of Jezebel and the level of spiritual warfare in these pages, Christian friends may mock and scoff. You might be considered by some to be "a little too religious." This should be no surprise, as even many "seasoned" Christians have determined they are "too spiritual" to be attacked by Jezebel, and convinced that if the spirit of Jezebel were truly at work in their church or lives, they would know.

It is interesting to note that the wisest man ever to walk the face of the earth, Solomon, was seduced by women who worshiped Baal. In 1 Kings 11:5-6 (NLT), we read: "Solomon worshiped Ashtoreth, the goddess of the Sidonians, and Molech, the detestable god of the Ammonites. In this way, Solomon did what was evil in the LORD's sight; he refused to follow the LORD completely, as his father, David, had done."

A woman who served Baal (the Jezebel spirit) was instrumental in the fall of Solomon. *No one* is immune to the attacks of Jezebel. In fact, if you believe you are too strong to fall to her, it is most likely you have already begun to be seduced by her. This spirit will not stand by and allow you to be delivered without a fight. She is made for war. She is ready to fight. Are you?

Note

All the stories in this book are true! Names and places have been changed to protect those involved, and to allow time for those who have operated in the Jezebel spirit to repent and change for the glory of God!

CHAPTER 1

WHO WAS JEZEBEL?

One woman brought down the kingdom of Israel. One woman sent the ministers and prophets of God running in fear for their lives. Her name was Jezebel. Jezebel was a seductive prophetess of the false god, Baal. We first hear about this infamous queen in 1 Kings 16:30-31 (NLT): "But Ahab son of Omri did what was evil in the LORD's sight, even more than any of the kings before him. And as though it were not enough to follow the example of Jeroboam, he married Jezebel, the daughter of King Ethbaal of the Sidonians, and he began to bow down in worship of Baal."

"WHEN AHAB, THE REIGNING KING OF ISRAEL, MARRIED JEZEBEL HE DIRECTLY ALIGNED GOD'S PEOPLE WITH GOD'S ENEMY."

When Ahab, the reigning king of Israel, married Jezebel he directly aligned God's people with God's enemy. It is remarkable that anyone would enter into a marriage or an alliance with a woman whose name means *without dwelling or cohabitation, unmarried, uncommitted or unhusbanded.* Jezebel will *not submit.* The word *unhusbanded* means, *to refuse to live in a peaceful cohabitation.* Jezebel was the daughter of a king-priest of Sidon named Ethbaal. *Ethbaal* means *man of Baal* or *with him is Baal.* He was a high priest of Astarte.

This is very important. Astarte was the Canaanite fertility goddess, also called Ishtar. In the Babylonian pantheon, this deity was the daughter of the moon god, Sin, and later the consort of Anu, the deity of heaven. She is usually regarded as the goddess of love and sensual pleasure or fertility. The Assyrians also fostered her identification as the goddess of war.

This is where it gets interesting. This high priest of Baal, Ethbaal, personally mentored his daughter in the heathen worship of this pagan god of sexuality and spiritual war. This king who was entirely devoted to Baal, indoctrinated his daughter with the notion that she was an ally of Baal, and her goddess of fertility is not only the giver of life but also the giver of death! He gave her the assignment of bringing death and destruction to all those who opposed Baal. Accordingly, he named her Jeze-Baal, (jĕz'ə, bəl), or Jezebel.

It didn't take long before the well-trained goddess of war began to manipulate the weaker Ahab into bowing down in worship to her Baal (1 Kings 16:31). As the king goes, so goes a nation. Now the Children of Israel who once bowed their knees to Yahweh (God) were fully engaged in Baal worship. In 1 Kings 16:32-33 (NLT), we read: "First Ahab built a temple and an altar for Baal in Samaria. Then he set up an Asherah pole. He did more to provoke the anger of the LORD, the God of Israel, than any of the other kings of Israel before him."

As part of the wedding arrangements, Ahab made provision for Jezebel to continue her worship of Baal. He even built her a temple to Baal—that's it, no big deal. He just created a space and a place for the anti-Yahweh god to reside.

Take note of this great lesson from the life and leadership of the weak, intimidated Ahab—the lesson of *compromise!* Ahab was already engaged in compromise by continuing the calf worship introduced by the king before him, Jeroboam, for 1 Kings 16:31 (NLT) says, "as though it were not enough to follow the example of Jeroboam." It is interesting to note also that Jeroboam was simply a servant of Solomon. After Solomon was seduced by beautiful women into worshiping Baal, God took the kingdom away from him and gave it to his servant, Jeroboam.

> Then he said to Jeroboam, "Take ten of these pieces, for this is what the LORD, the God of Israel, says: 'I am about to tear the kingdom from the hand of Solomon, and I will give ten of the tribes to you! But I will leave him one tribe for the sake of my servant David and for the sake of Jerusalem, which I have chosen out of all the tribes of Israel. For Solomon has abandoned me and worshiped Ashtoreth, the goddess of the Sidonians; Chemosh, the god of Moab; and Molech, the god of the Ammonites. He has not followed my ways and done what is pleasing in my sight. He has not obeyed my decrees and regulations as David his father did.'" (1 Kings 11:31-33, NLT)

Solomon warned himself of this very situation but still had to learn his lesson firsthand. In Proverbs 17:2 (NLT), we read: "A wise servant will rule over the master's disgraceful son and will share the inheritance of the master's children."

Solomon lost his kingdom over compromise, and Jeroboam did the very same thing! Now Ahab took compromise to a whole new level with his alliance with Jezebel. This young prophetess of Baal now held the seat of absolute power as queen over Israel. She not only established the worship of Baal, but she instituted one of the first ever recorded persecutions of followers of Yahweh (God). Jezebel's reputation spread as her regime quickly set to work murdering the only people who would speak against her and her pagan practices: God's prophets. Those who escaped with their lives went into hiding in fear of her. In 1 Kings 18:4 (NLT), we read: "Once when Jezebel had tried to kill all the Lord's prophets, Obadiah had hidden 100 of them in two caves. He put fifty prophets in each cave and supplied them with food and water."

Once the prophets of God or anyone else who dared to oppose her were removed, Jezebel hastily put together an army of her own prophets. Her staff numbered 450 prophets of Baal and 400 prophets of the goddess, Asherah. Over 850 loyal servants now taught Baal worship and practices to the Children of Israel, enforcing its practices. Israel was all hers and due to her efforts, the worship of Baal was embraced by the people as "normal."

Baal worship was the ultimate rejection of God. The God who created the universe was made to watch His greatest creation (people) worship something that they had created. Baal worship is a form of self-worship. And it gets worse! *Baal* means *master, possessor* or *husband*. Yahweh was "master and husband" to Israel. He called Israel His bride. "Husbands, love your wives, just as Christ loved the church and gave himself up for her to make her holy, cleansing her by the washing with water through the word, and to present her to himself as a radiant church, without stain or wrinkle or any other blemish, but holy and blameless" (Ephesians 5:25-27). Israel was divorcing God for a new master, Baal.

The worship of Baal rejected the holiness set up by Yahweh (God) and encouraged indulgence in every self-pleasing sexual desire as a part of self-worship. Through the worship of Baal came the god *Dagon,* for Baal was the son of Dagon. Baal, Dagon, Ashtoreth, and Molech combined for the erotic acts of perverted heterosexual relations, homosexual activity, violent sexual acts, body piercing (including genitals), body cutting, and an infatuation with blood (drinking and draining), prostitution, and ceremonial orgies. They were also one of the originators of child sacrifice. Sadly, God's children were participating in all this debauchery and His prophets were being chased off from doing anything about it. With her rebellious, manipulative practices installed in the culture, only a fraction of the Jews that remained still lived their lives in covenant with God, according to some theologians.

Jezebel and her god, Baal, stood in direct opposition to Yahweh. It was of utmost importance for her to elevate Baal and the worship of him in Israel. Her god didn't have to be the true God, he just had to be an option. Jezebel knew that when the prophet Elijah confronted her prophets of Baal, her gods would neither be able to bring fire from heaven nor display true power.

> Then Elijah said to them, "I am the only one of the LORD's prophets left, but Baal has four hundred and fifty prophets. Get two bulls for us. Let them choose one for themselves, and let them cut it into pieces and put it on the wood but not set fire to it. I will prepare the other bull and put it on the wood but not set fire to it. Then you call on the name of your god, and I will call on the name of the LORD. The god who answers by fire—he is God." (1 Kings 18:22-24, NIV)

"THE PURPOSE WAS NOT FOR JEZEBEL'S GOD TO ANSWER BY FIRE, BUT TO GET HIM ON THE SAME STAGE AS THE TRUE GOD. "

The purpose was not for Jezebel's god to answer by fire, but to get him on the same stage as the true God. Jezebel will force her way onto the stage because she wants Baal to be on the same altar as God. Jezebel's influence was so powerful that even Elijah, who had called down fire from heaven in his confrontation of over 850 prophets of Baal, ran for his life and prayed that he "might die"! All this was due to one woman simply threatening him.

When Ahab got home, he told Jezebel everything Elijah had done, including the way he had killed all the prophets of Baal. So Jezebel sent this message to Elijah: "May the gods strike me and even kill me if by this time tomorrow I have not killed you just as you killed them." Elijah was afraid and fled for his life. He went to Beersheba, a town in Judah, and he left his servant there. Then he went on alone into the wilderness, traveling all day. He sat down under a solitary broom tree and prayed that he might die. "I have had enough, LORD," he said. "Take my life, for I am no better than my ancestors who have already died." (1 Kings 19:1–4, NLT)

Elijah went from watching God send fire from heaven—experiencing one of the greatest manifestations of God's power ever—to running for his life, ultimately asking God to take his life! This is an example of the demonic power that Jezebel walked in. After God displayed Himself on Mt. Carmel and demonstrated His power, it did not diminish Jezebel's zeal for Baal—in fact, it amplified it.

Jezebel continued to dominate God's people and led them with evil, malicious, self-gratifying behavior. A prime example of this was when she manipulated others to murder a man named Naboth (1 Kings 21:8-14). Jezebel did this to get for herself a vineyard he owned and had refused to sell to King Ahab. This unscrupulous action affected all Israel and undermined the throne of Ahab. It sparked a prophetic revolution and the extermination of the house of her husband, Ahab.

It would be years before a man named Jehu would finally confront Jezebel and bring a stop to the idolatry and witchcraft she had brought to the house of Israel. Jehu had a determined, warring spirit. Jezebel did her best to intimidate Jehu, but she could not manipulate him. In 2 Kings 9:30-31 (NLT), we read: "When Jezebel, the queen mother, heard that Jehu had come to Jezreel, she painted her eyelids and fixed her hair and sat at a window. When Jehu entered the gate of the palace, she shouted at him, 'Have you come in peace, you murderer? You're just like Zimri, who murdered his master!'"

Jehu did not back down. He ordered Jezebel's own servants to throw her down from the tower balcony. When they went to find and dispose of her body, she was found completely dismembered by animals. In 2 Kings 9:36-37 (NLT), we read: "When they returned and told Jehu, he stated, 'This fulfills the message from the LORD, which he spoke through his servant Elijah from Tishbe: "At the plot of land in Jezreel, dogs will eat Jezebel's body. Her remains will be scattered like dung on the plot of land in Jezreel, so that no one will be able to recognize her."'"

Finally, the tyranny of this evil queen was brought to an end. As is often the case with the most infamous villains, though Jezebel was dead, there still persisted among them an eerie feeling that she might not be gone for long. Though Jezebel was dead, never to be seen again, the spirit that influenced her behavior was alive. In fact, it is still very much alive and real today. Over the course of this book, we will look through the entire Bible and various current day examples to see the many ways this same spirit manifests through people.

Jesus's words in the New Testament (Revelation 2:20) were, "Nevertheless, I have this against you: You tolerate that woman Jezebel who calls herself a prophetess." (See Revelation 2:20-26 for context.) Theirs was toleration of the spirit by the ignorance of it. I believe that the *spirit* behind the woman, Jezebel, is the very same spirit at work in many individuals today. This spirit is bringing the same destruction to God's house, the Church, through compromise, self-worship, immorality and a removal of the prophetic voice (prophets). Now that you know a little bit about the person of Jezebel, let's look more closely at how the spirit behind her influences people through the actions and characteristics they display in their everyday interactions and behaviors.

Dealing with Jezebel: Do's and Don'ts

Do: Always listen to your God-given discernment and wisdom.

Don't: Don't compromise with Jezebel.

CHAPTER 2

RECOGNIZING JEZEBEL'S CHARACTERISTICS AND BEHAVIORS

It's amazing to me that I can talk to a pastor in the South, a worship leader in the Northwest, or a prayer intercessor in the Midwest and they all report experiencing the same Jezebel characteristics and behaviors in various individuals. They can be seen in fellow Christians, pastors, church members, family members, bosses, coworkers, and more. When I've described the characteristics of the spirit of Jezebel, I've often had people tell me, "You're describing my leader, in-law, church member, or friend down to a T!" Many times, I've been able to practically finish the stories they tell me. How am I able to do that? Why do all these people who have never met act so eerily similar? Because it's not a person we are dealing with; it's a *spirit*. It's time to expose some of Jezebel's behaviors and characteristics. See if any of these characteristics ring a bell.

Warning

As I list these behaviors and characteristics I will use the terms "she" and "her," but remember, this spirit is no respecter of gender nor limited to any particular type of person. *This spirit operates in men and women alike.*

Another caution: Note we are in *no way* on a witch hunt to try and find the spirit of Jezebel in everything and everyone. There are varying stages of the Jezebel spirit. Some individuals are being introduced to the spirit and begin developing her characteristics, while others are more deeply affected and become fully mature in the spirit. No one characteristic means that someone is operating in a fully developed Jezebel spirit. But those who exhibit multiple characteristics and behaviors listed, you can be confident that the Jezebel spirit is at work in them to some degree. At the same time, this spirit (as you will learn) is a power hungry, controlling spirit that moves in witchcraft to manipulate people through intimidation, sex, control, and many other tactics. I believe it has become common for this wicked spirit to attack the Body of Christ. So yes, it might relate to a few people!

Let's get to know Jezebel.

Behavioral Characteristics

She is dominant.

Domination is Jezebel's main M.O. (modus operandi, or method). She must be in full control. She gets what she wants at the expense of anyone or anything. She is forceful and overbearing. She will talk over you, ignore you, and devalue you so that she is the only one who appears valuable, important, or in a place of power.

She is mean-spirited.

Jezebel is just mean. You cringe when you're around her and you hear the things she says to people and about people. There is no reason for her to be so unkind, but she is. She bears no fruit of the spirit. In Matthew 7:20 (NKJV), we read, "Therefore by their fruits you will know them." Only at times does she pretend to like people, let alone love them. But even when she is doing nice things for people, it's quite often with wrong motives.

She is jealous of everything!

Jealousy is a primary motive for her behavior. She has to be the *best at everything*. She needs to be the best singer, pray the best, be the best-looking, have the deepest insights, have the greatest revelation, be the wealthiest, be the most important and so on. So if anyone else excels in any of these areas it plunges her into a state of jealousy. Anything there is for her to be jealous of, she will be.

If the attention of others should turn from her to you, prepare to feel her wrath. Jezebel was the queen and had her every natural need met, but that wasn't enough; she wanted the only spot of land that wasn't for sale. She was jealous over what she did not have, so she took it. In 1 Kings 21:4-7 (NLT), we read: "So Ahab went home angry and sullen because of Naboth's answer. The king went to bed with his face to the wall and refused to eat! 'What's the matter?' his wife Jezebel asked him. 'What's made you so upset that you're not eating?' 'I asked Naboth to sell me his vineyard or trade it, but he refused!' Ahab told her. 'Are you the king of Israel or not?' Jezebel demanded. 'Get up and eat something, and don't worry about it. I'll get you Naboth's vineyard!'"

Jealousy in the Group

Beth was a prayer intercessor who loved God and loved her pastor. She felt a burden to pray for him and did so on a daily basis. Eventually, Beth's pastor recognized her call to intercessory prayer ministry and asked her to be a part of his personal intercessory prayer team at the church. Beth had always prayed for the pastor and his family but she also knew the power that the Bible teaches when we pray in unity with others. Beth felt truly humbled to be a part of the church's prayer team and accepted her pastor's request with excitement.

The first time she met with the group, she found the group's leader, Kathryn, far from welcoming. Kathryn was extremely jealous of Beth and the bond she had formed with the pastor. By her actions, Kathryn quickly made it known to Beth that she was unwelcome and her prayers were not only unnecessary but damaging to the pastor and the church.

Then Kathryn began to sabotage Beth's reputation aggressively. She would not tell Beth about scheduled meetings with the pastor, and then when she didn't show up, would tell the pastor, "Beth wasn't really committed to the church or called to pray for you." Before services, Kathryn would lock the door to the room the prayer team prayed in so that Beth couldn't join the team to pray. During pre-service prayer, Kathryn would follow Beth while she prayed. Beth could hardly think straight or pray the way she wanted to; it was like a demonic force behind her, it was so intimidating. It messed with her head! Beth could not focus to pray.

Beth started going to prayer very early to get there before Kathryn so she could pray alone for a while. So Kathryn started going earlier also and told Beth, "You aren't allowed to be there alone." James 3:16 became a reality for her, "For wherever there is jealousy and selfish ambition, there you will find disorder and evil of every kind." It got worse and worse.

Kathryn began to tell Beth that her prayers were hurting the pastor and his family and that when she entered the church, demons would follow her. Kathryn would frequently come up to Beth during service, hold her by the hand and pray insulting, derogatory things over her. Beth was so hurt by the things Kathryn was saying and doing that she finally went to talk to her pastor. When Beth met with her pastor, she was surprised to find out that for months Kathryn had been warning him about Beth, expressing all the same concerns Beth had with Kathryn! The church was growing so fast that the pastor didn't have the time or energy to deal with the problems with a few ladies on a prayer team. He decided that it would be best if Beth stepped down from the prayer team. Beth was crushed and told her pastor, "I pray for you because I love you, not because I'm on a prayer team!" Beth was removed from the prayer team but never stopped praying for her pastor.

With Beth's removal, problems continued on the prayer team. The pastor eventually dismantled it entirely. The spirit of Jezebel continued to attack the church, the pastor, and his family. He left the church a few years later. Kathryn no longer attends a church of any kind and Beth still prays for her former pastor and his family every day!

She is charming and knows how to turn on the sweetness.

Jezebel is so fake! It's as if she can turn on an entirely different persona at will—of sweetness. In fact, it's not a different persona, it's a different *spirit* and sounds different, but it's all the same. She's not genuine and you know it. She's only sweet because she wants something from the person she is trying to win over. For example, when she hugs you, you want to cringe because you know it's not genuine, but you just press through the awkwardness to be polite. Either she is being sweet to gain favor or to move into a greater position of power or authority. She will butter you up to throw you off the trail of her real motives.

She is the expert and knows more than anyone.

Jezebel is the untrained expert of everything! Don't worry if you don't have the answer—she does. She will be quick to inform you she has all the answers and you need her for future answers. She will talk over you. She will discredit and belittle the opinions of others to make them sound inferior and unwanted. She says things like, "Oh, okay, thanks for that idea, yeah, mm-hmm, that's great," to brush people off before they can finish a sentence. She probably couldn't repeat a single thought or idea just expressed by another because she wasn't listening! She just can't wait for others to stop talking so she can.

She does what she wants, without permission.

Since Jezebel is unhusbanded, "married but un-submitted," she will not submit to natural authority. If she does cooperate with authority, say with a pastor or ministry, it is merely because she is trying to gain influence and power within that ministry until she can execute her real plans and motives. Jezebel will start unsanctioned ministries, Bible studies, events, prayer meetings and gatherings outside the governing authority and protocol of the church. Then when she is confronted by church leadership, she gives an amazing excuse, or tells people quite a story: "I only wanted to help people," "I can't believe a church would not want more prayer, Bible studies, or so on." By doing this, she gains influence with her listening audience and plants seeds of rebellion, discord, and offense in the hearts of her listeners, who then wonder why the church would do what they did to her.

She stirs up strife.

Jezebel stirs up strife, creating opposition against people or ministries. Those who operate in strife will stimulate, entice, move, provoke, and persuade people to their destructive personal agenda. Jezebel stirs people up in an unhealthy way, often through gossip and slander. She will tell people information about others simply to create strife in their hearts towards one another. She will share negative information about pastors or church leaders "just so you can pray for them," attempting to cloak her gossip and slander in a prayer request. What she is truly doing is sharing information to plant seeds of strife in people influenced by a church or ministry. Strife involves going to people and telling them any information that will harden their hearts towards another person or ministry.

She is a planner.

Jezebel is quite often ten steps ahead of you. Every conversation, meeting, interaction, prayer, and compliment has a motive behind it. Even if the person operating in this spirit is unaware of exactly what she is doing and why, the spirit leading her knows exactly what it's doing every step of the way. She has a master plan and is executing every detail, down to coming up with her littlest comments and planning with whom to share them. She plans her provocative comments, knowing that immature hearers particularly will respond to them in such a way that they will appear to be the ones with the issues, not her. Her plan is to hijack your ministry and your spiritual fruit. This is why it's important that you know what God has called you to do and have a clear vision (plan) for your life. It's nearly impossible to *out-strategize* her. Responding biblically is always the best course of action. God will defend you best that way.

She is savvy and sly, using flattery to seduce the fleshly and weak-spirited.

Jezebel thinks of herself as being very savvy; skilled at concealing her true motives. When she says something that is completely wrong, she thinks no one can discern it because of how smoothly she says it. She is always careful to present her views with all the right intentions, and from the purest of motives. Her slyness is the key to her strategy for seducing the spiritually weak. She loves to teach others how to be savvy and sly as well, mentoring them to be just like her. When caught in her savvy attempts to maneuver, she often responds by saying, "You just misunderstood my real heart!"

She cannot take no for an answer.

When you say no to her, she perceives it to be a personal assault. The word "no" creates boundaries. Jezebel is not submissive and will not honor boundaries. "No" is a declaration of war for her. You *cannot* disagree with her without experiencing the repercussions of her complete wrath. Not only can you not say no, but she will accept nothing less than a yes, and will do all in her power to force one from you. You will find yourself constantly agreeing with Jezebel to avoid the war.

When you prepare to meet with her, you can go over your thoughts and rehearse exactly what you will say until you are blue in the face but still come away from the meeting totally mixed up and somehow in agreement with her! You will catch yourself always feeling as if you are supposed to give in to her or feel sorry for her. Saying yes to her is even worse than the inability to say no to her. You don't know how it happens, but you inexplicably end up agreeing to what she puts before you! Be careful. You can even end up agreeing with her without saying yes, simply by being unable to say no!

She hates those who won't cater to her!

If you don't fall in line, you will quickly find yourself on Jezebel's "hit list." She can and will make your life miserable very quickly. If you do not cater to her and how she wants you to run things, she will go out of her way to let you and everyone else know how much you are not wanted or needed around anymore.

Her playground is your emotions.

Jezebel will mess with your emotions constantly. She will use any tactic necessary to get you to a state of dependence upon her. She uses bribery, sexual favors, pouting, fake tears, weeping, emotional outbursts—whatever it takes—to put you in a defensive position so that you can never confront her or move on past her.

People influenced by Jezebel tend to bring up everything they have ever done for you. They want you to feel emotionally indebted to them. Not much is done out of the goodness of their heart. They will frequently remind you of how you owe them!

Jezebel is the queen of crying on command. This woman (or man), can turn on the waterworks whenever necessary to escape confrontation or opposition. This is a tactic of manipulation. She knows it is hard to talk about the real issue when she seems upset (even to the point of tears), so she distracts you with emotion. The tears are a smoke screen.

She gives blanket statements like, "I was only trying to do my best!" (Deep breath. A second deep breath.) "I mean, I only wanted to help!" Never mind grabbing a tissue. She wants you to see that hers are real, streaming tears. Invariably, her victims back down and say something like, "Well, I can see you're really upset. Let's just talk about this some other time." But it is most likely that he or she will not enter Jezebel's emotional playground again.

Jezebel must be first.

Jezebel demands to defend herself. Just as a child runs to her parent to tell her side of the story first, Jezebel always wants to be the first to tell her side of the story. Since she is so manipulative, it reaches the point where it comes off as downright childish. You will find that she will be quick to call the leader, family member, mutual friend (whoever the third party mediator is), to tell her side of the story first. Well, every good parent knows that the child that runs to tell his or her story first is usually wrong and hiding something. In Proverbs 18:17 (NLT), we read, "The first to speak in court sounds right— until the cross-examination begins."

The Worship Leader Meltdown

David was on staff at a large church. One Sunday he had a run-in with a coworker of his, one of the worship leaders. Just after a worship service, David ran into him in the back hallway and asked him why he had used his designated office space for his event for the worship department without his permission. It was a simple question, but the worship leader blew up at David, yelling at him as the pastor delivered his sermon in the sanctuary nearby.

David was concerned people in the congregation would hear, but the worship leader was unconcerned. With huge tears welling up in his eyes, his hands on his hips, he asked David sarcastically, "Do you own this property?" David was incredulous, finding it hard to believe this was really happening. He held his tongue, doing his best to be respectful as this gentleman had been in ministry at the church longer than he. Then David responded, "Can we just have a mature, adult conversation?"

At that, the worship leader stormed off dramatically, waving his hand in the air, talking to himself, pausing every ten steps or so to turn back towards David, point his finger and say, "We're done here!" He refused to talk to David! It finally reached the point where the worship leader got in his car and left the building before the service even ended. This presented a problem as he was the primary piano player, scheduled to play for the end of the service altar time.

David found himself standing alone in the back hallway, looking down both ends of it, asking himself, "Did that really just happen?" David knew that this unprofessional behavior needed to be brought to the supervising pastor's attention. David waited for the service to end and for the people to clear out before he called the supervising pastor on his way home from church. Before David could tell him what had happened, the supervising pastor informed David that the worship leader had already called him. Not even an hour had passed and the worship leader had already called to tell the supervising pastor his side of the story! The spirit of Jezebel will childishly defend herself.

She likes to talk.

Jezebel does not stop talking! "Too much talk leads to sin" (Proverbs 10:19, NLT). She usually has a quick answer for everything, albeit an inaccurate one, unable to hold up against even the simplest rebuttal. To avoid contradiction, she resorts to simply keep talking over you. She always seems to have an answer for everything (no matter how ill-reasoned). Jezebel will make up new policies on the spot to manipulate meetings and conversations. If you ask to see those policies in writing, they are nowhere to be found. Watch her wiggle and squirm when you continue to ask the same question, demanding specifics and truthful answers.

She has no fruit of the spirit.

Jezebel bears no results of the presence and work of the Spirit—its fruit—as detailed in Galatians 5:22-24: "But the fruit of the Spirit is love, joy, peace, patience, kindness, goodness, faithfulness, gentleness and self-control." Those who belong to Christ Jesus have crucified the sinful nature with its passions and desires. Out of all the fruit of the Spirit, Jezebel's greatest deficiency is that of self-control. There is no evidence proving her to be a self-controlled person living a crucified life. From sexual desires to sinful indulgences, there is no fruit in her life! Not only does she have no fruit, but she destroys the fruitfulness of others.

She does not love.

You won't feel love from Jezebel because there is none in her. Jezebel loves herself, her agenda, and her will. Since she serves herself, you will never feel the love of God from her. Why? Because she doesn't love God. This is proven by the way she treats God's people. Just because someone bears a title that indicates he or she works for God or a church does not mean he or she has the heart of God to love others.

Jesus questioned one of His loyal workers three times, asking him if he truly loved Him. In John 21:17 (NLT), we read: "A third time he asked him, 'Simon son of John, do you love me?' Peter was hurt that Jesus asked the question a third time. He said, 'Lord, you know everything. You know that I love you.' Jesus said, 'Then feed my sheep.'" Just because Jezebel works for a church or calls herself a Christian does not mean she holds the love of the Father in her heart. She loves with selfish love and will turn on you in a second. Her demonstration of love is manipulative and conditional: "I'll do this for you if you do this for me." This is not true, godly love.

Information is her ammunition.

Don't tell her *anything!* Whatever you tell Jezebel, she will use against you. She will take things you tell her in confidence and use them to try and discredit you publicly. Jezebel draws information from people. She will constantly seek information she can use to sound and appear to be intuitive, spiritual, and factual. She will use the information you give her in false prophecies, making it sound as if she is speaking from God. She will make provoking statements and ask questions like: "You've really been on my heart; are you okay?" and, "Why don't you tell me what's *really* going on? You can trust me." To disclose personal information to her about your struggles and weakness will merely arm your future enemy with what she perceives to be spiritual strength. Trust me, later on you will ask yourself: "Why did I say that? Why did I tell her that personal information?" Remember, Jezebel draws it out of you only to use it against you.

Twisting the Truth

Josh was a minister who excelled in leadership within his denomination. He had been through some rocky situations but had remained faithful in building God's house. However, the leading elder at their church was heavily influenced by the Jezebel spirit.

At one point, Josh confided in the elder, sharing a problem he had faced in the leadership of a previous church they had worked for and personal challenges they had faced in early days of ministry. He shared his experience in being forced to transition from one ministry to another due to mishandled funds, immorality, affairs, and divorce among the previous church's leaders. Josh had gone through a difficult process, having taken a stand for righteousness while facing significant intimidation from the errant leaders.

The entire time Josh was sharing all this with the elder, he grew more and more uneasy about it. Afterwards, he almost felt guilty. In the back of his mind he knew he had made a mistake.

Later, the elder in whom Josh had confided used the information he shared with him to try and damage Josh's ministry and reputation. When Josh would not agree with or submit to the Jezebel spirit in operation within him, he twisted the truth and told every pastor he could that Josh had been unfaithful in serving in churches over the years, and attempted to make it appear he was the "real" problem as he had a "history of defiance."

"...JEZEBEL USES INFORMATION AS AMMUNITION."

This elder attempted to use personal information Josh shared with him in confidence to manipulate him. This is just one example of how Jezebel uses information as ammunition.

She works in confusion.

Confusion is Jezebel's platform for manipulation. You will never know where you stand with her because she keeps you in a constant state of confusion on this. One minute you think everything is great. The next minute, everything falls apart and you feel her wrath.

God clearly teaches us that He is not the originator of confusion, so when it enters your life, be mindful that the spirit of Jezebel may be in operation. (We will look closer at confusion in chapter 4.)

She is the queen of humiliation.

Jezebel will humiliate anyone who rises against her. She does this through belittling, bullying, lying, sabotaging, and emasculating. Jezebel takes on a dominant, masculine persona. She does this to intimidate the true leaders that could challenge her.

In ancient warfare, physical emasculation (removal of testicles) of an enemy was used to terrorize the rest of the enemy's forces, to strike fear in them. The idea was to so humiliate them that they would have no confidence to rise up against you. This is what Jezebel does spiritually through emotional humiliation. By doing so, she takes authority over people, especially male leaders that threaten to resist her or expose her weaknesses.

This tactic is also used in marriages when an overbearing wife humiliates her husband by sharing with others that he has failed to provide for her or the family or how he fails to fulfill her sexually. This humiliation gives her the upper hand (control) in the relationship because he doesn't want his weaknesses to be exposed.

She is a projector.

Jezebel will project upon others what is actually in her. This is one of her primary tactics. She is quick to "see" and point out negative behaviors and characteristics in others, accusing them of being prideful, having wrong motives, being unloving or untrustworthy, and more. Why? Because she is all these things, she "sees" them in others and makes malicious accusations to keep attention from their operation in her own life. By projecting these negative traits on others, she keeps them so busy defending themselves and clearing their names that they (and any audience she can find for her accusations) are distracted from the evil at work in her.

She loves money.

People say money is power, but perhaps no one believes this more than Jezebel. The truth is, money provides a false sense of power. Jezebel serves false gods, so it only makes sense she is drawn to money. She uses money to control and manipulate, lording it over people. She gives gifts with strings attached. Jezebel works hand in hand with the spirit of mammon (as we will see in Chapter 10).

She is sexually immoral.

Jezebel hates the righteousness of God. She lives a carnal, immoral, seductive lifestyle. She also encourages this behavior in any way she can. She seeks to defile the holiness of God. (We detail Jezebel's sexual tactics in Chapter 9.)

Relationship Characteristics
She has no accountability!

Jezebel hates godly discipleship, mentoring, and healthy, balanced relationships. She is not accountable because she is deceptive in her true intentions. Because she refuses to submit to God, she cannot submit to any man or leadership. She might appear to be submitted, but as with anyone, her submission level is only revealed when her will is challenged. For example, If I give my daughter whatever she wants, her submission is untested. It is when my will contradicts hers that her ability to submit is tested. Resisting accountability encourages rebellion. Jezebel is drawn to the rebellious.

"RESISTING ACCOUNTABILITY ENCOURAGES REBELLION. JEZEBEL IS DRAWN TO THE REBELLIOUS."

She creates soul ties.

Jezebel is your best friend...that you just met. She establishes an overbearing attachment in a very short period of time. She tries to jump into deep relationships fast. She does this to try and gain a higher level of trust, without the proper foundation of an authentic relationship. You feel close to her and think you can trust her. She probes the soul with statements like: "Are you okay? I've had this burden for you lately." She won't ever challenge you to ask the Lord for answers or learn to hear from Him as she wants you to just hear from her. She uses people and calls it "mentoring."

She uses people.

People become Jezebel's human shields. She will get others to do her dirty work so she can say, "I did nothing wrong!" "Then two scoundrels came and sat opposite him and brought charges against Naboth before the people, saying, 'Naboth has cursed both God and the king.' So they took him outside the city and stoned him to death"(1 Kings 21:13). She used the scoundrels to carry out her own agenda.

She is so sly she will get others to voice her opinions and carry out her plans. If there is ever a blowup, her hands will be clean. She lets others take the fall.

She needs you to need her.

Jezebel needs to be needed. She never helps you overcome anything, she just makes you need her more. In spite of all the time you spend with her, you will notice you never seem to overcome any of the issues you share with her. She keeps you dependent upon her, emotionally. She wants you to think she's the only one who understands. She never has real answers, but you will notice you spend more and more time together. She will get you to doubt your faith, replacing it with anxiety!

She is vindictive.

She rejoices in the sufferings of those who stand in her way! In 1 Kings 21:7 (NIV), we read: "Jezebel his wife said, 'Is this how you act as king over Israel? Get up and eat! Cheer up. I'll get you the vineyard of Naboth the Jezreelite.'" She said, essentially, "Rejoice, I've just murdered and stolen to get you what you wanted!" She rejoices in the fall of others. *Be careful of this!* If you rejoice when others fail, you *do not* have the heart of God and it is most likely Jezebel is trying to gain influence in your life and ministry.

> Don't rejoice when your enemies fall; don't be happy when they stumble. For the LORD will be displeased with you and will turn his anger away from them. (Proverbs 24:17-18, NLT)

> Don't repay evil for evil. Don't retaliate with insults when people insult you. Instead, pay them back with a blessing. That is what God has called you to do, and he will bless you for it. (1 Peter 3:9, NLT)

> You have heard the law that says, "Love your neighbor" and hate your enemy. (Matthew 5:43, NLT)

What Was On That Paper?

A life-changing moment for Dustin came during a church service as he watched his mentor, one of the most influential men in his life, minister one night. As he exhorted the church, Dustin noticed he seemed unusually emotional, almost angry. He continued ministering and encouraged the church, saying the Lord would fight their battles for them.

As his mentor led the congregation back into worship, Dustin saw him throw a piece of paper on the altar and then stomp on it! It immediately captured Dustin's attention. Dustin didn't think anyone else noticed, but wasn't sure. When Dustin saw this incident, his spirit was alarmed.

As soon as Dustin was able, he picked up the piece of paper as discreetly as he could. He later opened up the crumpled paper to see what it was. It was a newspaper clipping, an obituary of a man who had once worked alongside his mentor. He had died that week. Dustin's mentor and this man had a falling out a few years prior that had ended with a severed relationship. Dustin's mentor had stomped on the picture of the man. He was so bitter; he had celebrated the man's death. Dustin was mortified! This was the most vindictive behavior Dustin had ever witnessed in his life.

She is obsessive.

Obsession is a common characteristic in unhealthy relationships. Jezebel exhibits a possessive, obsessive love, and then becomes spitefully vindictive in a "bipolar-like" fashion, displaying roller-coaster emotions. Ridiculous numbers of emails, text messages or back-to-back phone calls (without leaving messages) can be attributed to her obsessive behavior. Infringing on people's personal space and family time is an obsession. Not allowing people to have other close friendships or mentors are other obsessive behaviors of Jezebel. Obsession is often seen in romantic relationships when the two people involved have been sexually active outside the holiness of marriage. It is an outward demonstration of the manifestation of the spirit of Jezebel. More than anything, Jezebel obsesses for power.

She is a queen of treaties.

Jezebel is the queen of false peace instead of covenant relationships. She never makes true amends, so she makes treaties to buy her time until she gets what she wants. *Jezebel married Ahab as part of a treaty*, to keep him in check. This is how she keeps people in check even today, with treaties, but not genuine peace. The thing about treaties is that one side always gets the upper hand to determine when to break the treaty and continue the battle. Don't forget, she is the goddess of war.

What's The Treaty For?

Chris was at odds with his mother, Anna. The entire family was long-time Christians, but struggled with unforgiveness. Chris had tried to make peace with his mom on numerous occasions, but it seemed like peace could never be made. Chris was just learning about the Jezebel spirit. Finally, Chris had a conversation with his mom to try and find resolution and make peace. As the conversation went on, it was clear Chris's mom would not soften her heart. At one point, she even tried to abandon the conversation and bring it to a quick end. She said, "We just need a treaty!" Chris was blown away! He told her, "A treaty! Why would we need a treaty when we are not at war?"

She is simply dysfunctional in relationships.

Jezebel cannot have healthy relationships because she is toxic. Every relationship she has is dysfunctional in one way or another. The majority of her relationships are at varying levels of strain, and she leaves a trail of devastation in her path. When she destroys one relationship, she will be quick to make amends (a treaty or false peace) with someone with whom she has had a broken relationships so it appears as if she has fewer shattered relationships than she actually does. She demands complete loyalty but gives none in return. Loyalty is not blind, it's godly!

Jezebel overprotects those under her so they will never grow or learn properly, insuring they will always need her. Jezebel trains

"LOYALTY IS NOT BLIND, IT'S GODLY!"

her children and spiritual children through manipulation and deal-making, not discipline and true discipleship. She bribes them into obedience rather than train them to be obedient.

Spiritual Characteristics
She resists the things of the Spirit.

Jezebel loves what God hates and hates what God loves. She hates repentance, humility, intercessory prayer, and true moves of the Spirit. She will begin to reveal herself whenever there is a genuine move of God. This is where she will break from her savvy demeanor and begin to expose her true heart. Jezebel cannot stay quiet when there is a true move of the Spirit of God. She will stop at nothing to silence the prophetic.

"JEZEBEL LOVES WHAT GOD HATES AND HATES WHAT GOD LOVES."

Stopping a Move of God

Nathan worked as the chaplain at a large church in the south. The church also had a school. A revival broke out in the school. Kids were getting baptized with the Holy Spirit, speaking in tongues. It was a genuine move of God. One day at lunchtime, hundreds of teenagers had gathered in the sanctuary to pray. Nathan was on the stage ministering, when his assistant came up to him and whispered in his ear, "The principal wants you to stop ministering and let the kids share." They were in the middle of a powerful, prophetic move of intercession. Due to Nathan's lack of experience and understanding of the Jezebel spirit, he just kept going. A few minutes later, his assistant came to him again and said the same thing, but added, "Right now!" Nathan could tell he was nervous. His assistant knew what God was doing, but their boss had essentially told them to shut it down. Nathan had difficulty navigating the moment, so he just kept going. He didn't have the option to stop and think it through. He didn't want to be disobedient, but he knew that God was doing a work in the students. Surely, the principal could see the power of God touching the students. They were on their faces before the Lord, all over the auditorium. Finally, the assistant principal came on stage and said to Nathan, "Per the principal: Stop now!" At that, Nathan handed him the microphone and walked off the stage. As he walked off, he saw the principal standing at the back of the sanctuary with her arms crossed, just watching him. Why would anyone stop an outpouring of the Holy Spirit on young people? No one would. Only a spirit would— the Jezebel spirit.

She is hyper-spiritual.

She can preach, pray, and prophesy better than anyone; she'll make sure you know it. In fact, she'll make sure everyone knows who she is. The Bible warns that she calls herself a prophetess (Revelation 2:20). We should take notice of 1 John 4:1 (NLT), which reads: "Dear friends, do not believe everyone who claims to speak by the Spirit. You must test them to see if the spirit they have comes from God." She is very spiritual! She regularly says things such as: "I was up all night, praying for you!" and, "You've really been on my heart lately." That's a lie! You haven't been on her heart. She just tells you this so that you will trust her, confide in her, and need her.

Since she usurps authority, she has no problem disregarding the authority of biblical prophecy. She will tell you she has a prophetic word for you, rather than allow you to judge if the word is truly prophetic (from God). She will use "prophecy" to manipulate individuals publicly, putting them in socially awkward situations. She will "prophesy" very generic "words," then put people on the spot and ask them publicly if the prophecy was from God, without allowing the proper procedure for evaluating it. She will regularly confirm her own prophecies rather than allowing prophets to do it and keep her accountable (1 Corinthians 14:29). In her attempts to be spiritual, she doesn't act as she should, according to the Bible. This is proof her spirituality is not from God.

She sows discord.

Discord causes disunity. Unity is very important in every family, marriage, church, leadership team, and business. Every team needs unity to accomplish the task at hand effectively. Discord breaks the ties of unity so that the team becomes weak. Ecclesiastes 4:12 (NLT) reads: "A person standing alone can be attacked and defeated, but two can stand back-to-back and conquer. Three are even better, for a triple-braided cord is not easily broken." Imagine a three-cord rope. Now imagine someone purposely cutting one cord of that rope. The remaining two cords will not have enough strength to hold the weight they were designed to hold and the whole rope will break. This is what happens when someone sows discord of any kind on a team. The individuals left trying to hold the weight break under the pressure.

The Pharisees sowed discord between Jesus and His disciples. In Matthew 15:1-2 (NLT) we read: "Some Pharisees and teachers of religious law now arrived from Jerusalem to see Jesus. They asked him, 'Why do your disciples disobey our age-old tradition? For they ignore our tradition of ceremonial hand washing before they eat.'" Notice that the Pharisees ask Jesus about the disciples' behavior, then later, they question the disciples about Jesus's behavior, in Matthew

9:10-11 (NLT): "Later, Matthew invited Jesus and his disciples to his home as dinner guests, along with many tax collectors and other disreputable sinners. But when the Pharisees saw this, they asked his disciples, '"Why does your teacher eat with such scum?"'" The Pharisees sowed discord by going to Jesus when they had a question about His disciples and going to the disciples when they had a question about Jesus. They did this to try to break the unity of their ministry.

Jezebel sows discord in a very subtle way. She uses words of suspicion that cause those young in faith to stumble. She makes statements such as, "I'm not sure what it is, but I just discern something bad about that person!" Consider that statement for a moment. It could appear to be genuinely protective and discerning, but in reality, it is deceptive and destructive. Those to whom Jezebel says these things are typically unaware of her motives and play right into her hand. They too want to be discerning, so instead of objectively discerning their behavior, they try to find the fault in that person (which is often not there at all). In Proverbs 6:16, 19 (ESV), we read: "There are six things the LORD hates—no, seven things he detests....A false witness who speaks lies, And one who sows discord among brethren." The Lord hates this behavior.

If Jezebel had truly discerned anything bad about someone, she would have been able to call it out. Of course, if she told you what she discerned, she would be sowing seeds of discord, as sharing something derogatory about someone else is not the right, biblical thing to do. She often makes negative and critical remarks about friends, family, and those serving in leadership. She'll say things like: "I love the pastor, but he's horrible at _____ (this or that)," following it up with, "but he would tell you this himself," as if this makes it appropriate to share.

She is a faultfinder.

This might be the most sinister characteristic of Jezebel; in fact, this was the first characteristic I learned about the Jezebel spirit. Since she projects onto others what is really in her, she will find fault in everyone who disagrees with her or comes against her. Notice that she will not mention *any* of these faults before she is opposed, but afterwards, she will unleash all her accusations. She will say things such as: "They have a bad heart," and "They were never really committed." She will compose faults according to her victim's personal weaknesses. If there is not actually a fault there, she will place one there. (Chapter 10 deals with this topic extensively).

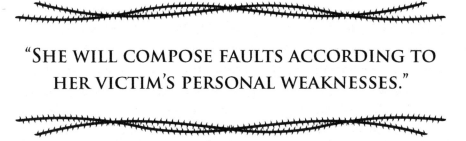

"SHE WILL COMPOSE FAULTS ACCORDING TO HER VICTIM'S PERSONAL WEAKNESSES."

She cannot and will not accept apologies.

This one puzzled me for a while. I couldn't figure out why those under the influence of the Jezebel spirit would never accept my apology. This was another major insight God used to reveal the spirit of Jezebel coming against my own life. My wife and I would apologize to people over and over and over—to the point it was like apologizing to a wall! It seemed as if every time they caused a conflict due to their Jezebel behavior, I was the one that ended up apologizing! I also noticed that even after I apologized, they remained hard-hearted and used the same things I had already apologized for as accusations against me. I was dumbfounded. This exposes how those influenced by Jezebel have a very hard time forgiving.

Over the years, I saw this scenario play out a number of times until I finally asked the Lord: "Why do those with a Jezebel spirit never accept an apology? Why do they continually bring up the same accusations?"

The Lord responded by asking me a question in return. He said, "What is forgiveness?"

"Letting go," I responded.

Then the Lord said, "Yes, letting go of control."

Forgiveness is letting go! If Jezebel forgives you, she has to let go of the control she has over you—something she will not do!

She is never, ever, ever wrong!

One of the greatest indicators that someone is operating under the Jezebel spirit is he or she will *never* admit to being wrong. From making excuses to faultfinding, he or she constantly defends his or her behavior and positions. Jezebel refuses to humble herself. She can't be wrong because the flesh leads her. She can't repent to God because she isn't submitted to Him. She resists Him and His leading to repentance. (Humility and the ability to repent keep us in right standing with God.) The bottom line is, she cannot be wrong. So even if you catch her being one hundred percent wrong on something, she'll never admit it. Why? She is just too prideful!

On occasion, I've even seen people under the Jezebel spirit make pretentious admissions of guilt, strategically pretending to show remorse momentarily, but only to quickly revert back to a prideful disposition. Jezebel is never, ever, ever wrong!

"JEZEBEL IS NEVER, EVER, EVER WRONG!"

She has no conscience.

Jezebel has no remorse for whom she hurts. It's amazing how some people think, as Jezebel does, that they protect their church by hurting the people in it. She claims to be simply defending her church, though thinks nothing of hurting God's people in the process. She has no remorse for her actions because they are all intentional. She hurts people on purpose. She uses people, and she destroys lives. Even if she is called out for exhibiting behavior that is obviously contradictory to the Word of God, she will merely respond by saying, "My conscience is clear."

Paul teaches us that just because we have a clear conscience, it does not mean we are in right standing with God. In 1 Corinthians 4:4 (NIV), we read: "My conscience is clear, but that does not make me innocent. It is the Lord who judges me." I've heard people boldly say, "I can sleep just fine at night," as if being at peace with themselves has to do with anything! The Bible shows us the *conduct* that brings us into right standing with God, not our *conscience*.

"THE BIBLE SHOWS US THE CONDUCT THAT BRINGS US INTO RIGHT STANDING WITH GOD, NOT OUR CONSCIENCE."

Leadership Characteristics
She is an answer to prayer.

Jezebel is an answer to prayer, a perfect fit for your ministry—at least she tells you she is. She will directly and indirectly make sure you know how much you need her. She will tell you: "You are doing way too much. God sent me as an answer to your prayers and to take burdens off you." Most importantly, she will constantly remind you how much you need her skills to help you grow your ministry or organization.

You will think that inviting her to help you was your idea! Basically, she will position it as if you asked her to help when really, she inserted herself. Her real motive for "helping you" is to gain more and more authority in your ministry so she can eventually control it. Pastors and leaders, be very aware you will make spiritually compromising decisions whenever you do so out of need. *You don't need her.* You need God to provide and He always will.

She loves the limelight.

Jezebel is a power hungry controller. She seeks positions of authority in leadership. She gains these positions by outperforming and undermining everyone in order to get close to people of power (whose power she will try to usurp). She must receive credit for everything she does. After all, it was her idea, and she heard from God. She is convinced that nothing in the ministry would succeed without her; in fact, the ministry itself would be *nothing* without her! She micromanages everything and everyone. She is quick to hire and fire. Goals are her priority, not people. She will run people off without a second thought. She will never go after a "lost sheep" though. She doesn't want to take care of sheep (people). She only wants people to serve her and her agenda.

All roads run through her.

If you can control the traffic into a kingdom, you can control the kingdom. Jezebel positions herself so people can never go over her head to someone above her. She controls the flow of information so that nothing that would expose her can get to her supervisor. She uses the excuse that she is protecting the leader or pastor, when in actuality, she is using them. She speaks for the leader or pastor, but nothing she says sounds quite like them. Don't get caught removing a roadblock around her or you will be charged with treason, because according to her, "the pastor (leader) told me" to set up all those roadblocks.

Absalom did this to King David. We read about it in 2 Samuel 15:2-4 (NLT): "He got up early every morning and went out to the gate of the city. When people brought a case to the king for judgment, Absalom would ask where in Israel they were from, and they would tell him their tribe. Then Absalom would say, 'You've really got a strong case here! It's too bad the king doesn't have anyone to hear it. I wish I were the judge. Then everyone could bring their cases to me for judgment, and I would give them justice!'"

She leads through intimidation.

She wants to be feared, not loved. Fear is control, and she can't release her control. She keeps it firmly in her grip. She leads through fear and intimidation while appearing innocent. (Chapter 3 deals more with this topic.)

She loves allies.

When confronted, Jezebel seeks allies and never responds properly or appropriately to correction. She utilizes the mob mentality to employ the "us against you" strategy: "If there are more of us in agreement than you have, obviously you must be wrong." (Remember, Jesus was often greatly outnumbered.) She never follows biblical principles of accountability when responding to correction or handling conflicts and disagreements. Nope, she gets to people first (usually alone), convincing them of her side of the story. She repeats this process until her alliance outnumbers yours and you succumb to the size of her army, either giving up or giving in. Directly or indirectly, she will say: "All of us can't be wrong; it has to be you!" or, "If you don't do what I say, all these people will leave you!"

She aborts her spiritual children.

Jezebel worshiped Baal with child sacrifice. Today, Jezebel will always sacrifice on the altar of religion the spiritual sons and daughters of the church or ministry. She will attempt to chase off all spiritual sons and daughters until, like Elijah, they must run for their spiritual lives. This is the sad end for the majority of victims who encounter the spirit of Jezebel within a church. They get chased off. They just can't take it anymore and leave due to pressure, pain, confusion, and anxiety. So the pastor loses spiritual sons and daughters and is left with the power hungry controller that sacrificed them on the altar of the religion of Baal. (Chapter 8 expounds on this characteristic.)

Dealing with Jezebel: Do's and Don'ts

Do: Always have someone with you when you meet with or confront Jezebel. Under no circumstance are you to meet with her alone.

Don't: Don't accept any gifts or personal favors from Jezebel.

CHAPTER 3

JEZEBEL'S WEAPONS OF WAR

This chapter exposes the method of Jezebel's witchcraft, and that is control. Her tactics for controlling individuals are fear, manipulation, intimidation, and domination. We will explore biblical and practical examples of how witchcraft wages war on the souls of God's people. Witchcraft incapacitates its victims. It completely drains them so they won't have the strength to continue to fight it and finally end up giving up on everything.

It's very important for you to understand that witchcraft is simply about controlling the will of another person. A rebellious person will directly or indirectly try to control others. Consider the spells performed by real witches, warlocks, and witch doctors. They are spiritual incantations designed to influence or manipulate people through demonic power. Jezebel uses the same form of witchcraft, but her spells are "words from God" used to control people. The Bible clearly teaches us the power of our words.

> The tongue can bring death or life; those who love to talk will reap the consequences. (Proverbs 18:21, NLT)

> And the tongue is a flame of fire. It is a whole world of wickedness, corrupting your entire body. It can set your whole life on fire, for it is set on fire by hell itself. People can tame all kinds of animals, birds, reptiles, and fish, but no one can tame the tongue. It is restless and evil, full of deadly poison. Sometimes it praises our Lord and Father, and sometimes it curses those who have been made in the image of God. (James 3:6-9, NLT)

Words are powerful. Let's look at one example of this from the music industry. In the summer of 2008, a pop artist and former minister's daughter came out with a song titled, "I Kissed a Girl." The song was very catchy and the arrangement was well-done. Teenagers across America sang her lyrics all summer long. The song describes a young girl who engages in drinking alcohol (assumed), becomes daringly rebellious, and explores her bisexual curiosity. She reassures her listeners that it's just human nature to experiment. She then describes the taste, the touch, and the emotions of kissing another girl and liking it!

These words encouraged a generation into bisexual curiosity and "bravery." Teens across the country tried kissing members of the same gender. They did this because—who knows—they thought they might just like it! Those lyrics and many like it are laced with *witchcraft*, and they manipulate minds, hearts, and spirits of a younger generation. In fact, spiritually, in the hearts of our young people, I believe this song helped lead the way for them to support the legalization of same-sex marriage and adopt a secular, anti-biblical stance on marriage.

I am *not* one of those ministers that calls the latest pop singer the Devil, the Antichrist, and so on. For decades, ministers have declared music artists to be evil. They said this about Elvis, Madonna, and now, artists such as Lady Gaga. In fact, I believe that God loves all these artists and that He sent His Son to die for them. However, I also believe that out of their *rebellion* they are used by the enemy (the Devil) to sing songs that have devastated the lives of millions of people.

To me, the scary thing is that some Christians support and endorse this music. They post on social networks how much they "love their music" and attend their concerts. They do this under the banner of love. They say, "We need to show artists like this the love of God." I agree...just not to do it at the expense of truth! There are two sides to love: grace and truth. The spirit of Jezebel wants us to abandon the truth side of love so we can believe her lie. Do not mistake judgment for discernment. The Bible tells us not to judge those outside the church (1 Corinthians 5:12). But to embrace this kind of worldliness is to abandon wisdom.

"THE SPIRIT OF JEZEBEL WANTS US TO ABANDON THE TRUTH SIDE OF LOVE SO WE CAN BELIEVE HER LIE."

Jezebel violates the will of her victims. Free will is incredibly important, and few people understand it. God created free will— He created us with a choice to love Him. God allowed Adam and Eve to choose to obey Him or not (Genesis 2). People have a hard time answering the age-old question, "Why do bad things happen to good people?" The answer is, God gave us free will to choose... and we chose to fall and bring sin into a perfect world, making it imperfect. In Deuteronomy 30:19 (NLT), we read: "Today I have given you the choice between life and death, between blessings and curses. Now I call on heaven and earth to witness the choice you make. Oh, that you would choose life, so that you and your descendants might live!"

God never violates our will. Jesus never violated anyone's will. The Holy Spirit will never violate your will, but Jezebel will violate your will through witchcraft. *Witchcraft chooses for you.* Witchcraft is illegitimate authority masquerading as authority from God. Jezebel controls through four main tactics: fear, manipulation, intimidation, and domination. Let's learn about them and how they operate.

Fear

The Bible teaches us about fear. In 2 Timothy 1:7 (NLT), we read, "For God has not given us a spirit of fear and timidity, but of power, love, and self-discipline." If God hasn't "authorized" us to be fearful, who has? Jezebel! The word for *fear* here, in Greek, is *deilía*. *Fear* is a feminine word that means *timidity, fearfulness, cowardice, caused by evil.* So why are you so afraid of this person operating under the Jezebel spirit? It's due to a *spirit of fear!* She incites fear primarily through threats. You end up responding to her threats rather than responding directly to her or the situation at hand. Threats are very distracting. They could cause you to respond to Jezebel rather than doing what God has instructed you to do.

Look at the fear inflicted by a threat on the prophet Elijah:

Now Ahab told Jezebel everything Elijah had done and how he had killed all the prophets with the sword. So Jezebel sent a messenger to Elijah to say, "May the gods deal with me, be it ever so severely, if by this time tomorrow I do not make your life like that of one of them." Elijah was afraid and ran for his life. When he came to Beersheba in Judah, he left his servant there, while he himself went a day's journey into the desert. He came to a broom tree, sat down under it and prayed that he might die. "I have had enough, Lord," he said. "Take my life; I am no better than my ancestors." (1 Kings 19:1-4, NIV)

She sent a messenger of fear with a threat. She didn't even deliver the threat herself. It was a third party threat. I want you to see how powerful witchcraft is. There is no evidence in the Bible of Elijah and Jezebel ever meeting face-to-face. Still, he felt the impact of witchcraft even through a messenger. Under the anointing Elijah had just confronted 850 false prophets and challenged them publicly (1 Kings 18). Fire had fallen from heaven, and Elijah put all 850 of them to death. Then *one woman* simply threatened him via messenger, and he ran away in the spirit of fear!

Let's get this straight: Elijah was afraid of Jezebel's death threat... so he prayed that God would take his life? He ran from death but asked for death? The spirit of fear will cause you to *run away* from where you're supposed to be—the ministry to which God has called you, your church, and your life's purpose.

"THE SPIRIT OF FEAR WILL CAUSE YOU TO RUN AWAY FROM WHERE YOU'RE SUPPOSED TO BE..."

If Jezebel had truly wanted to kill Elijah, why did she send a messenger instead of an assassin? If the messenger found him, couldn't a trained killer? She didn't want him dead—she wanted him paralyzed in fear. She didn't want him dead—she wanted his faith dead, his anointing dead, and the prophetic dead. Jezebel wants you alive because if you're alive, you can be controlled!

Her curses come in the form of threats. She declares them over your spirit and soul. She uses words, letters, accusations, and emails to threaten. Her threats of fear sound like this: "If you don't do what I say, everyone is going to leave your church/ ministry/business and you'll be left with nothing!" or, "If you leave *this* church, God will never use you! You will fail wherever you go. You will not prosper!" These threats demand a challenge.

We preach to drug addicts, alcoholics, prisoners, the sexually deviant, and everyone else, that they can come to Jesus for a new life. We say that no matter what they've gone through, God can heal them, free them, and deliver them. Her threat suggests if they leave a certain *ministry*, God will never use them again. It doesn't make sense! But when a Jezebel says it, somehow people believe it! Why? It's due to a spirit of fear! She makes people think that if they separate from her or her ministry, they are separating from God! Hear this: *Jezebel doesn't determine whom God blesses!*

"Jezebel doesn't determine whom God blesses!"

Manipulation

The second tactic of control is manipulation. Jezebel is undisciplined, so she must manipulate. She manipulates through pouting, sulking, the silent treatment, possessiveness, tantrums, sexual favors, withholding sex, withholding money, threats of suicide, guilt, affliction of mental or physical torment, and more. She will bring up your past mistakes, failures, or other personally sensitive areas to manipulate you. She will get you feeling sorry for her through self-pity so you will cater to her.

You see this in family situations. A family member crosses a very sacred boundary, possibly with sexuality. It could be a husband who cheats on his wife or a family member who molests a child and then tries to make the victim feel sorry for him or her because of the consequences he or she will suffer. Often they are successful in causing people to feel sorry for them. This is a Jezebel spirit and it is using a key strategy—*manipulation!*

Unfortunately, I've been in meetings where I had to confront an individual's sinful behavior. More than once after these meetings, these people have manipulated me with sob stories, trying to make me feel sorry for them as they hurt others. It is important to stand firm for righteousness and defy the manipulations of Jezebel.

Jezebel will manipulate in every way imaginable. To show she is more important than everyone else, she will put on quite a show of always being busy and in a hurry. She will say things such as, "We need to talk, right now," but never tell you what you need to talk about. She will call an "important" meeting, change the time or day multiple times, and then cancel it moments before it is scheduled to begin, letting you know you can "meet in a few weeks." This causes your anxiety to grow over a longer period of time. She manipulates a move of the Spirit in services, often through false prophecy and giving her own self-serving interpretations. Most of all, she will *manipulate the Word of God!* She will try to use the Bible to hurt people. This is never okay!

"USING THE BIBLE TO HURT PEOPLE IS WITCHCRAFT!"

Using the Bible to hurt people is witchcraft! The Word of God brings life, not death. Even when the Holy Spirit brings rebuke or instruction, it is always with grace, in love. In Hebrews 12:6 (NLT), we read, "For the LORD disciplines those he loves, and he punishes each one he accepts as his child." Jezebel uses the Word to break people. She twists the Scripture for her agenda, making it appear that God is on her side, warning that He will punish you if you cross her. Remember this: Anytime you pray against people, *it is witchcraft!* We are never to pray against people! However, we are to pray against the spirits that influence people. In Ephesians 6:12 (NLT), we read, "For we are not fighting against flesh-and-blood enemies, but against evil rulers and authorities of the unseen world, against mighty powers in this dark world, and against evil spirits in the heavenly places." It's a spiritual battle, not a battle of the flesh.

Intimidation

The third tactic of control is intimidation. In 2 Kings 9:30-31 (NIV), we read, "Then Jehu went to Jezreel. When Jezebel heard about it, she put on eye makeup, arranged her hair and looked out of a window." She painted her eyes to make them look bigger, to overawe (restrain or subdue) Jehu, and to intimidate. This tactic with eye paint was a two-part strategy; physical intimidation and seduction. Professional athletes do this. They paint their faces and put black lines around their eyes to appear more intimidating to their opponents. Jezebel intimidates so no one will stand up to her.

The spirit of Jezebel was active through Goliath. In 1 Samuel 17:8-11 (NLT), we read: "Goliath stood and shouted a taunt across to the Israelites. 'Why are you all coming out to fight?' he called. 'I am the Philistine champion, but you are only the servants of Saul. Choose one man to come down here and fight me! If he kills me, then we will be your slaves. But if I kill him, you will be our slaves! I defy the armies of Israel today! Send me a man who will fight me!' When Saul and the Israelites heard this, they were terrified and deeply shaken." The Israelites were intimidated at even the thought of standing up to the Jezebel spirit operating in Goliath.

Jezebel intimidates through mockery. She will publicly mock you and laugh at you to stir up insecurity in you. We see this many times in Scripture. In Nehemiah 2:19 (NLT), we read: "But when Sanballat, Tobiah, and Geshem the Arab heard of our plan, they scoffed contemptuously. 'What are you doing? Are you rebelling against the king?' they asked." In Acts 2:4, 13 (NLT), we read: "And everyone present was filled with the Holy Spirit and began speaking in other languages, as the Holy Spirit gave them this ability....But others in the crowd ridiculed them, saying, "They're just drunk, that's all!" People use mockery to intimidate and try to stop the move of the Holy Spirit and the will of God.

People tried to intimidate Jesus through mockery. Mark 15:17-20 (NIV) reads: "They put a purple robe on him, then twisted together a crown of thorns and set it on him. And they began to call out to him, 'Hail, king of the Jews!' Again and again they struck him on the head with a staff and spit on him. Falling on their knees, they paid homage to him. And when they had mocked him, they took off the purple robe and put his own clothes on him. Then they led him out to crucify him." They mocked Jesus to try to get Him to abandon His assignment of the cross. It didn't work.

Jezebel verbally intimidates, saying things such as: "You don't have a clue what you're talking about," and "If you don't do what I say I will destroy your reputation!" She intimidates through demeaning, hurtful comments meant to damage your self-esteem. She constantly lets you know who you are *not* and your areas of weakness! She intimidates through mind games to prevent you from knowing where you stand with her. She says in many ways: "You'll never be as good as me. You will never have a larger ministry, be more successful, or exceed me in any way." You can never do anything right, and certainly not as well as she. Intimidation causes you to step back in fear rather than step out in faith.

Intimidating speech is a major tactic of a Jezebel. She uses belittling words such as "boy," "girl," "kid," "Who are you?" and more. She wants you to shrink in your faith so she can intimidate you with her spiritual "size." She doesn't want you to grow in God.

I Guess You're Not A Grower

Some time ago a pastor friend called me. He was extremely confused and upset due to intimidation from his church administrator. In a meeting the administrator had gone off on a long rant telling him: "You have to be a producer! You've got to be a grower! I'm telling you, boy, some people are just not growers, and I don't want to waste my time with anyone who can't grow a ministry!"

The church administrator was frustrated that the youth minis-try wasn't large enough. He wasn't concerned if the young people were being discipled or growing in their relationship with the Lord, he just wanted more youth in attendance! I told my friend that what his church administrator was saying was not biblical, and he was try-ing to intimidate him while pretending to motivate him. As we spoke, the Lord brought 1 Corinthians 3:6-7 (NLT) to my spirit: "I planted the seed in your hearts, and Apollos watered it, but it was God who made it grow. It's not important who does the planting, or who does the watering. What's important is that God makes the seed grow." The Bible clearly teaches that we are planters of the Word of God and nurturers of it. We are not growers. God is the grower.

At the end of the conversation, we prayed together for his church administrator. Over the course of time, we saw a real change in his church administrator and his heart turned to people over numerical growth.

Domination

The fourth tactic of control is domination. Domination results when the person under the influence of the Jezebel spirit has complete, 100 percent control over another person. Domination is a cultish leadership style. Those under the influence of the Jezebel spirit vio-lently enforce their will through complete dominance and power. A dominant leader's decisions, actions, and choices are not to be ques-tioned. If you try to question him or her, you will be crushed. You will be the cautionary tale for others to see, to discourage them from questioning.

This is why Jezebel likes to keep weak, needy people around her. Weak people will not rise up against her. Weak people won't bite the hand that feeds them.

Dominance is a result of a lack of submission and accountability. In fact, dominant leaders have limited accountability, if any! They sel-dom release people. They only draw people to themselves to use and abuse them. This is why a church will never grow in health if a Jezebel runs it. Under leadership influenced by Jezebel, people will never grow into who they are called to be. Jezebel needs them only to serve her agenda. She keeps people broken so they will continue to need her. She knows their weaknesses and how to keep them vulnerable. She uses humiliation to dominate their emotions and strip them of any confidence. Like a battered spouse, she makes others feel powerless to disagree with anything she does for fear of repercussions.

If Jezebel doesn't get her way, she'll make you pay! She taxes others emotionally until they can't take it anymore and will do anything to make peace. *Peace at any cost is spiritual terrorism!* Such peace delivers you to her domination.

"PEACE AT ANY COST IS SPIRITUAL TERRORISM!"

Be cautious of ministries led by families. This doesn't apply to *every* family ministry, but occasionally it is the case. Ministries run completely by one family tend to put family members before anyone else at the cost of compromising the integrity of the ministry. Where there are people there will be disagreements; where there are disagreements there will be conflict. Our biblical integrity will be determined by how we respond to conflict. Ministry families get in trouble when they put a family member above the Word of God by justifying unethical conduct and covering up sinful behavior to protect the family's reputation. Eli the high priest did this when he refused to confront his sons' evil behavior. As a result, the prophetic mantel was taken from him and given to a teenager named Samuel (1 Sam 1-3).

If there is no outside accountability to submit to, such ministries are a breeding ground for a Jezebel spirit to dominate! This can be easily prevented with the proper implementation of unbiased accountability from outside the ministry family.

Some of you have had the Spirit of Jezebel viciously oppose you. If you have encountered her witchcraft, I encourage you to boldly pray this prayer out loud:

Father, in the name of your son, Jesus, I come to you, recognizing the tendencies that I have to think I need someone to control me, show me, or place responsibility for me so that I don't have responsibility. Father, would you heal me from this tendency? Would you heal me from my susceptibility to control and manipulation? Father, would you heal me of needing something so badly that I allow someone else to get it for me versus allowing you to bring it to me?

Father, I have replaced you with someone else in my life and that someone has taken advantage of me. I ask you to remove these issues and help me to be totally dependent on you. And Lord, from this day forward, may I never be susceptible to control and manipulation. May I never walk in fear of failure. May I never walk in any fear but the fear of you. May I be able to see clearly and not through the eyes of another, but through the eyes you give me.

I recognize your incredible love for me. I recognize that you are transforming me and know this is a part of the process as I leave this chapter of my life. It will be left behind. It will never exist again because you God, are great and awesome. Remove it to the farthest sea, away from me, never even to be remembered.

I cast myself before you, Lord, asking you to cleanse me from all unrighteousness. Cleanse me from all adultery. Cleanse me from my own personal shortcomings and fear. May we walk together the rest of my life. May I have an impact on others, freeing them to walk in you as well.

May your name be glorified, for truly your kingdom is forever and I will be with you one day in the fullness of that kingdom. I ask this in the name of Jesus. Amen."

Dealing with Jezebel: Do's and Don'ts

Do: Always stand up for righteousness, integrity, and purity, no matter who comes against you.

Don't: Don't let Jezebel misuse or misquote Scripture to you or about you.

CHAPTER 4

EFFECTS OF WITCHCRAFT

Witchcraft is real. You may not be aware of it, but I assure you, you have felt the impact of it. Witchcraft spawns devastating effects that can go undetected for years, even by the most experienced Christian. The effect of Jezebel's witchcraft disarms her enemies spiritually, breaking them down by distracting them so they don't have strength to resist her any longer.

Fear

We explored fear and now we will examine the effects of fear. Fear paralyzes you. Fear stops you in your tracks—like a deer caught in the headlights, frozen as if in a trance. Fear keeps you from moving forward and going where God has called you to go.

In 1 Kings 19:9, we read, "And the word of the LORD came to him: 'What are you doing here, Elijah?'" God asks Elijah this because he wasn't where he was supposed to be. It's never a good thing when God has to ask you, "Why aren't you where I called you to be?" Elijah was not where God told him to be because he was running away from Jezebel, in fear. God knew that fear would keep Elijah from his destiny, holding him in the past, disabling his faith. It is the same for us. Paul reveals God's view of His people that abandon faith for fear in Hebrews 10:38 (NIV), "But my righteous one will live by faith. And if he shrinks back, I will not be pleased with him." God does not delight in your fear. It does not please Him.

Discouragement

Fear gives birth to discouragement and discouragement is the purpose of fear. Discouragement will cause you to keep your eyes on
every problem and off solutions. Discouragement can make your
problem seem bigger than God. Discouragement is one step short
of quitting. I can't emphasize this enough: *Jezebel wants you to give
up!* She wants you to give up on ministry, family, business, and life.
She wants you to give up before God raises you up. She doesn't want
you to fulfill the call of God on your life. She wants to silence the prophetic voice inside you. You need to take the phrase, "give up," *out
of your vocabulary!* When discouragement is full-grown, it develops
into depression.

"YOU NEED TO TAKE THE PHRASE, "GIVE UP,"
OUT OF YOUR VOCABULARY!"

Depression

Depression runs rampant across our nation. According to the Anxiety and Depression Association of America, of the over forty million
adults in the United States eighteen years of age and older, 18 percent
struggle with depression.[2] This is Jezebel at work, but we medicate
and treat depression as if it is only a mental disorder instead of what
it truly is, the work of our spiritual enemy. The number of Christians—
even pastors—fighting depression is staggering. The most common
treatment for depression is medication, but medication does not get
to the root of the issue. If you take medication to calm your mind
and emotions, then why do you need the Holy Spirit? In actuality,
the medication replaces the Holy Spirit. We get the word, *pharmacy,*

from the Greek word, *pharmakeía*, which comes from the word, *pharmakeuō*, which means *to administer drugs, drug-related sorcery, like the practice of magical arts.* Could it be the medication we take is not only replacing the Holy Spirit, but resisting the Holy Spirit? I believe it can and is. *You cannot win this spiritual battle with medication.* When you are depressed, you have no energy and no strength to fight. You don't care anymore, so Jezebel wins! Depression renders people hopeless. Some people have chemical deficiencies that cause depression and they have to supplement that chemical to correct depression. This is not the same as uncontrolled anxieties caused by not trusting in the Lord. As believers in Christ we know there is no such thing as hopeless for those who put their hope in Christ Jesus.

And so, Lord, where do I put my hope?
My only hope is in you. (Psalm 39:7, NLT)

Elijah found himself sliding into depression. He was falling farther and farther down. He was in a low place. As we see in 1 Kings 19:3-4 (NLT), depression caused this godly, spiritual man to feel so worthless, hopeless, and useless that he wondered if life even mattered, and became hopeless: "Elijah was afraid and fled for his life. He went to Beersheba, a town in Judah, and he left his servant there. Then he went on alone into the wilderness, traveling all day. He sat down under a solitary broom tree and prayed that he might die. 'I have had enough, LORD,' he said. 'Take my life, for I am no better than my ancestors who have already died.'" If depression is coming against you, know that you are not "crazy"! You are feeling the physical, mental, and emotional effects of the spirit of Jezebel.

Anxiety

Anxiety is a very common effect of witchcraft, and unfortunately, I have personally experienced it many times. When an anxiety attack hits you, it feels like you just ran a marathon. You can barely breathe. The best way I can describe it is, it feels like someone has literally reached down your throat and ripped the breath straight out of you.

A Demonic Experience

I remember a time when my pastor asked me to go and pray over the workplace of a businessman in the church. I called the man and we made plans to meet the next morning. I asked a minister from the church to go with me.

When we arrived, the businessman brought us into his messy office. He had purchased an entire three-story building downtown and was remodeling it. He told us there were ghosts in the building and asked us to do an exorcism. He said his dog would not go up the stairs to the second floor because of these ghosts. This man had only recently begun attending the church and wasn't very mature spiritually. I also discerned that this gentleman had not fully submitted himself to the Lord. I could see darkness in his eyes. Matthew 6:22–23 (NLT), reads: "Your eye is a lamp that provides light for your body. When your eye is good, your whole body is filled with light. But when your eye is bad, your whole body is filled with darkness. And if the light you think you have is actually darkness, how deep that darkness is!" Out of the corner of my eye I saw a box of what appeared to be pornographic DVD's— right there in his office (Jezebel). I knew then that this man welcomed darkness into his life. The man proceeded to tell me that the building had been a government housing project known for substance abuse, so "all sorts of people lived here, doing who knows what." I told him that I would go through his building and pray over it, dedicating it to Christ.

I took out a vial of anointing oil and began to anoint the building as I prayed in the Spirit. I walked the entire first floor without incident, but when I made my way to the second floor, I turned down the hallway and felt chills run through my body. I started to pray louder in the Spirit. As I rounded the corner to the far side of the hallway and entered into an apartment, something suddenly stole my breath away. I couldn't get air. I couldn't pray. I was engulfed in the strongest anxiety I had ever felt. I pressed with all my strength and prayed as loud as I could in the Spirit. I stood there with my eyes closed until I felt the peace of God come into the room.

Anointing that building and experiencing the physical effects of witchcraft as I had that day taught me how to sense when witchcraft is coming against me, which has proven invaluable in my life and ministry.

After that experience I became very aware of what a demonic force felt like physically. Later, I noticed that every time I encountered individuals who were influenced by the Jezebel spirit, I would feel a similar attack of anxiety. It's important to know you will *never become immune to the impact and effects of witchcraft*, but you can become mature and more capable of handling them.

> "...YOU WILL NEVER BECOME IMMUNE TO THE IMPACT AND EFFECTS OF WITCHCRAFT, BUT YOU CAN BECOME MATURE AND MORE CAPABLE OF HANDLING THEM."

In one of my discipleship sessions with my mentor, John Paul Jackson, I asked him, "When do you get over the Jezebel attacks so that you don't feel them anymore?" He responded humbly, as he always does, "I don't know, I'll tell you when I do!" Your mind will tell you that you should arrive at a place where you never feel the impact of a demonic attack. But remember that Jesus Christ himself felt the physical impact of a demonic attack. In Luke 22:44 (NLT), we read, "He prayed more fervently, and he was in such agony of spirit that his sweat fell to the ground like great drops of blood."

Ten Years Later

One day, out of the blue, Phil got a call from a pastor named Simon with whom he had worked in ministry years before. It had been ten years since they last communicated. After some small talk, Simon asked, "Do you still talk to Lee?" (Lee was the boss they had both worked for in that ministry.) Phil said he had not and then asked him why he was inquiring. Simon said he had received a random voice-mail from someone at Lee's office, asking him to call back right away. (Jezebel had held a powerful influence over Lee during their time of working for him.)

"You haven't talked to Lee in over ten years. Did you feel any anxiety when your secretary gave you this message?" Phil asked.

Simon responded immediately, "Oh yeah, almost immediately!"

"Wow," Phil thought. "My friend Simon hadn't talked to our old boss in a decade. Even now, as a successful pastor of a church of his own with over a thousand members, he gets one call and boom! All the anxiety he experienced in the past came rushing back!" This is a prime example of how anxiety can attack you at any age or level of spiritual maturity.

Confusion

Confusion is a primary effect of witchcraft. Confusion makes you think you're going crazy! Many of us can handle a lot but when we can't get a hold of our mind and thoughts, we begin to panic and break down. You will never know where you stand with Jezebel. She keeps people in a constant state of confusion. One moment you can think everything is great, only to feel in the next moment that everything is falling apart, especially when you feel Jezebel's wrath. It's amazing how, in one moment, someone can attend a church, love it, have no problems with it, and feel as if everything is great, only to engage in one conversation with a Jezebel that throws everything into uncertainty. They are left so *confused*! They are suddenly unsure about the pastor, everything in the church, and whether they should even be there. They don't know whom to trust. Predictably, they pull back from the church and press into their friend, Jezebel. Jezebel operates and flourishes in complete confusion.

One day you are going full-on for what you know God has called you to do. Then, after spending time with a Jezebel, you are so confused that it leaves you unsure you should be in ministry at all. The Bible teaches us about this spirit of confusion. In 1 Corinthians 14:33 (KJV), the Word assures us, "For God is not the author of confusion, but of peace."

We see this same spirit in operation in regard to people's sexuality. They use the phrase "confused" to determine their spiritual and mental state. God clearly teaches us that He is not the originator (author) of confusion, so when it enters our lives, Jezebel has ushered it in. Confusion and the Jezebel spirit work in conjunction with an Antichrist spirit. When you have not made your foundation firm in Jesus, the spirits that resist Jesus come against you. When we fix our eyes on Jesus and refuse to break our connection with Him, we can break the effects of confusion. In 2 Corinthians 4:18, we read: "So we fix our eyes not on what is seen, but on what is unseen. For what is seen is temporary, but what is unseen is eternal."

Symptoms Of Witchcraft

There are other less obvious symptoms of being on the receiving end of witchcraft. For example, fatigue is subtle but it can be a great distraction and hindrance. If you are always tired (even when you get enough sleep), and never seem to have enough energy, it can have a negative impact on your life. Worst of all, fatigue can leave you spiritually drained, without energy to pray or spend time with the Lord. Spending time in the Word just seems like a strenuous task when you feel spiritually drained. Fatigue will also cause you to be too tired to deal with Jezebel. You can't find the strength to confront the spirit, so you keep putting it off. All the while, she gains more and more power.

Finally, chronic illness is a sign of witchcraft. If you're constantly sick and the doctors can't seem to find any natural diagnosis for your sickness, it may be due to a spirit of infirmity through witchcraft. Many times, this spirit of infirmity will attack the pastor's wife and family when he is dealing with a Jezebel spirit in his ministry. The enemy will attempt to damage the family in order to distract the minister and destroy the entire ministry. It's crucial to remember to pray for your pastor's and leader's families on a daily basis.

Possession and Oppression

It's important to know there is a difference between demonic possession and oppression. Possession describes an individual (like Jezebel) who has completely succumbed to a demonic inhabitation, allowing a demonic spirit to reside within him or her, submitting full control to the spirit. Judas was an example of a man completely surrendering to the Devil. In Luke 22:3 (NLT), we read: "Then Satan entered into Judas Iscariot, who was one of the twelve disciples."

Oppression is an outward attack of demonic powers. Someone who is oppressed can feel the effects of demonic forces, but is still in the resistance stage. In James 4:7 (NLT), we read: "So humble yourselves before God. Resist the devil, and he will flee from you." The key to breaking free from oppression is to submit every area of your life to the lordship of Jesus Christ. Any area of your life that has not been submitted to Jesus is susceptible to demonic influence. In Ephesians 4:27 (NIV), we read, "and do not give the devil a foothold."

The name of Jesus is the highest authority. The name of Jesus is the authority to cast out demons. He gives us permission to use his name (authority) over every demonic power that comes against us. In Mark 16:17 (NIV), we read, "And these signs will accompany those who believe: In my name they will drive out demons; they will speak in new tongues." When engaging in spiritual warfare, it's important to be wise in all your actions. The best strategy is to use the Word of God to respond to the enemy, just as Jesus did (Matthew 4).

When experiencing the effects of witchcraft from the spirit of Jezebel, I encourage you to make sure you spend time in the presence of the Lord to renew your mind in the Word (Romans 12:2). Take a moment now to pray and access the authority of Jesus. Say this prayer out loud:

In the name of Jesus, I recognize this is not from heaven. These thoughts are not from heaven, these feelings are not from heaven, and these actions are not from heaven. I refuse them in the name of Jesus. The Bible says in James 4:7, if I resist, the Devil will flee from me. I recognize this is the Devil and I resist him and rebuke him. I command he will not come near me.

Now I speak to my spirit. I command my spirit to take control over these issues, just as the Holy Spirit in my spirit takes control of my life, my thoughts, my will, and my emotions. I will be conformed to do what Jesus would do in this moment. I refuse the attacks of the enemy and I accept what you, God, want for me. In the name of Jesus Christ. Amen.

Dealing With Jezebel: Do's and Don'ts

Do: Allow God's voice (the Word) to rebuke Jezebel's voice.

Don't: Don't let Jezebel lay hands on you or pray for you. Ever!

Chapter 5

Jezebel and Self-Deception

In this chapter, we will explore the way the spirit of Jezebel begins to operate in people and makes its way into families and churches through self-deception. Self-deception is the initial entryway for the Jezebel spirit to gain access, authority, and then power over your life. Self-deception blinds you to the thoughts and behaviors of the spirit of Jezebel that you are acting out.

"Self-deception is the initial entryway for the Jezebel spirit to gain access, authority, and then power over your life."

The Common Denominator

Over eight years, Danielle had been a part of the leadership team in three churches. All her departures were rocky at best. She was asked to leave by a few of the ministries and the other one was not amicable. All of the ministries had the same complaint about her. They all accused her of attempting to undermine the pastor and doing her own thing. Danielle had a hard time with authority and submitting to her pastors. In her own mind, she was right and the other pastors were all wrong. Danielle couldn't see her self-deception. She was convinced that she was wrongly accused, mistreated, and she made sure she let everyone know it. Danielle was quick to tell anyone who would listen that she had been mistreated by other pastors (an attempt to make people feel sorry for her).

After taking a break from ministry, Danielle became involved with a new church in a different city. She and her family loved the church. Danielle inserted herself into the church by getting involved. Shortly after being placed on the leadership team, her pastor called a meeting with her. He confronted her about numerous complaints he had been getting about her from many members in the church. People were complaining that she was controlling, manipulative, and attempting to take the ministry in a different direction than the pastor. The pastor told her, "there are just too many complaints to ignore." Danielle was shocked at these allegations and firmly stated, "These people just misunderstand me and don't know my real heart!" Danielle asked the pastor if she could go and talk to the people who made the complaints.

Her pastor knew she had a history of problems with leadership. He decided to test Danielle. He told her, "I'm going to give you an opportunity to show your real heart." Danielle was relieved. He said, "I want to make this extremely clear. I do not want you talking to any members on the leadership team or members of the church about any of this. If you go to one single person behind my back, then you will have exposed your true heart. Do I make myself clear?" Danielle agreed to the boundaries her pastor had set in place.

Danielle left the meeting and before even twenty-four hours had passed, began calling the people that complained to the pastor about her, disobeying and rebelling against her spiritual authority. Danielle was removed from leadership at the church. Danielle still couldn't figure out why her pastor had treated her as he had and removed her from leadership. She had convinced herself that she *was just misunderstood. She failed to see that she was the common denominator in every circumstance. Danielle was self-deceived!*

Jezebel desires to deceive the self-deceived! Self-deception gives the spirit of Jezebel unwarranted access into your life. You deceive yourself before she ever deceives you. Self-deception is a battle within your own mind, a war within your own heart. It's that battle against flesh and blood that is part of the war you fight to keep your heart soft so the Holy Spirit can lead and guide you rather than you simply leading yourself. So many Christians live out their Christianity being led by their own hearts. *This is not biblical!* We are not instructed to follow our heart, *we are instructed to guard our heart* (Proverbs 4:23)!

"JEZEBEL DESIRES TO DECEIVE THE SELF-DECEIVED!"

In Jeremiah 17:9, we read, "The heart is deceitful above all things, and desperately wicked: who can know it?" *Desperately wicked* is translated *incurable* in the Hebrew. *The Message* version of the Bible shows Jeremiah 17:9–10 as: "The heart is hopelessly dark and deceitful, a puzzle that no one can figure out. But I, GOD, search the heart and examine the mind. I get to the heart of the human. I get to the root of things. I treat them as they really are, not as they pretend to be."

We will always be able to talk ourselves into what we think is best for us. Self-deception starts when we think we know better than God! This is exactly the tactic Satan used to deceive Eve in the Garden of

Eden (Genesis 3). The Bible gives us the blueprint for our lives. It's our moral compass, our ethical guide. We are to lay down our belief systems, pick up the Word of God and allow it to be the lamp unto our feet and a light unto our path (Psalm 119:105).

Who can describe how wicked the heart is? How can we truly know our own heart until it is tested? King David was a man after God's own heart, but he allowed self-deception into his own heart. In 2 Samuel 11, King David makes a series of bad decisions. He wasn't at war where he should have been and ended up committing adultery, sleeping with another man's wife. She became pregnant and he tried to cover up his sin. When his attempts at that failed, he had her husband murdered so he could take her, Bathsheba, to be his wife. After all this happened, the prophet of Israel, Nathan, confronted David and his sin. We find the account of this in 2 Samuel 12:1-6:

> The LORD sent Nathan to David. When he came to him, he said, "There were two men in a certain town, one rich and the other poor. The rich man had a very large number of sheep and cattle, but the poor man had nothing except one little ewe lamb he had bought. He raised it, and it grew up with him and his children. It shared his food, drank from his cup and even slept in his arms. It was like a daughter to him. "Now a traveler came to the rich man, but the rich man refrained from taking one of his own sheep or cattle to prepare a meal for the traveler who had come to him. Instead, he took the ewe lamb that belonged to the poor man and prepared it for the one who had come to him." David burned with anger against the man and said to Nathan, "As surely as the LORD lives, the man who did this deserves to die! He must pay for that lamb four times over, because he did such a thing and had no pity."

David was self-deceived! He didn't even wait for Nathan to finish his story, he was in such a rush to declare judgment and sentence the offender to the moral justice he deserved. David was keen to see the sin committed by the man in the story, but not in himself. This is self-deception. Sin is sin. Self-deception always leads us to make ourselves out to be better than we are, and certainly better than others. In Matthew 7:3-5 (NLT), we read: "And why worry about a speck in your friend's eye when you have a log in your own? How can you think of saying to your friend, 'Let me help you get rid of that speck in your eye,' when you can't see past the log in your own eye? Hypocrite! First get rid of the log in your own eye; then you will see well enough to deal with the speck in your friend's eye."

Then Nathan pulled the rug from beneath him in 2 Samuel 12:7, telling David, *"You are the man!"* David was confronted with a matter of the heart. He was shown how he had let himself become deceived and drifted away from his relationship with a holy God. In 2 Samuel 12:13, we read: "Then David said to Nathan, 'I have sinned against the LORD.' Nathan replied, 'The LORD has taken away your sin. You are not going to die.'" There is always mercy for those who humble themselves and reject self-deception. David knew all too well how dangerous his own deceiving heart could be. He had fallen into temptation and become lost in self-deception. He learned his lesson and never wanted to become self-deceived again. That's why he prayed this in Psalm 139:23-24 (NLT): "Search me, O God, and know my heart; test me and know my anxious thoughts. Point out anything in me that offends you, and lead me along the path of everlasting life."

If you compare the lives of Saul and David, you will find that David has many more recorded sins than Saul. Saul was arguably a better natural father than David. So why was Saul remembered as a tyrant and David a hero? I believe it was a difference in how they dealt with self-deception. When Saul was confronted with his sin and self-deception, he rejected the rebuke by Samuel and rebelled deeper into deception (1 Samuel 15). David did the opposite when confronted with his sin and self-deception. He cried out for God to forgive him. The difference was *repentance*. This is why God said David was a man after His own heart (Acts 13:22). *A repentant heart cannot be a self-deceived heart.*

"A REPENTANT HEART CANNOT BE A SELF-DECEIVED HEART."

Learn to examine your heart and ask God to reveal the hidden sin that self-deception has allowed to be seeded deep within your heart (Psalm 36:1). Take time now to pray and search your heart:

Father, I humbly come before you. Jesus, I pray that you would intercede on my behalf to the Father. I ask you, Lord, to search my heart and by the leading of your Holy Spirit, reveal to me the areas I in which I have become self-deceived. Father, I know your Spirit is Wisdom and your Word says in James 1:5 that if we ask for wisdom, you will generously pour it out to all those without fault. Father show me my hidden sin, my faults and the areas in my life in which I have rebelled against you. Show me these areas I have hid from myself.

Lord, I come boldly to your throne and ask you to expose the areas in my life that have allowed me to entertain self-deception. Father, forgive me. Extend your mercy and grace to me. I declare and decree that no spirit but the Holy Spirit is welcome in my life. I ask you to give me the gift of discernment. Teach me how to hear your voice. Speak Lord, your servant is listening. Amen.

Self-deception begins to take root when a person entertains thoughts that are contrary to the Word of God. In Proverbs 21:2, we read, "All a man's ways seem right to him, but the LORD weighs the heart." A self-deceived person says things like, "My conscience is clear!" *Your clear conscience does not make you right in your standing with God.*

You can silence your conscience over time by continuing to ignore the voice of the Holy Spirit. In 1 Corinthians 4:2-4, we read: "Now it is required that those who have been given a trust must prove faithful. I care very little if I am judged by you or by any human court; indeed, I do not even judge myself. My conscience is clear, but that does not make me innocent."

Your conscience is not an infallible guide! Just because your conscience is clear doesn't mean you're right. It doesn't matter if you think it's right, you must ask yourself what the Word of God says. We are not the judge, God is. You don't need to be right in your own eyes or in the eyes of other people—you need to be right in God's eyes. The heart of every problem in man is the problem in his heart.

"YOUR CONSCIENCE IS NOT AN INFALLIBLE GUIDE!"

Unchecked pride allows self-deception into your heart. In Obadiah 1:3-4, we read: "'The pride of your heart has deceived you, you who live in the clefts of the rocks and make your home on the heights, you who say to yourself, "Who can bring me down to the ground?" Though you soar like the eagle and make your nest among the stars, from there I will bring you down,' declares the LORD." Dr. Alan Bullock notes, "Self-deception begins to form when a person strives for a high spiritual position while purifying his own selfish passions and begins to rely on his own judgment." You can become so consumed with being important and right that you lose the heart of God. You can win a battle (being right), and lose the war at the same time.

This is how Jezebel gets in. She keeps you so concerned with being right that you can deceive yourself into thinking everyone else is wrong. If you're right, you don't have to convince anyone—you sure don't have to convince yourself. If you have to convince people, you're probably wrong! It's not about winning with man, it's about being right in the Lord's eyes. In Proverbs 3:7, we read, "Do not be wise in your own eyes; fear the LORD and shun evil." Self-deception blinds you so you cannot see Jezebel coming. Humility keeps Jezebel and self-deception out of your life. David quickly repented and declared, "I've sinned!" That is what kept him a man after God's own heart.

Here is a list of red flag statements that indicate self-deception has made its way into your heart.

- "I'm just going to go with what my heart is telling me to do."
- "My conscience is clear. I can sleep fine at night."
- "I can't forgive them for the thing they did to me."
- "I'm not religious and you have a religious spirit on you."
- "We're married in God's eyes."
- "I plan on making things right, later."
- "This issue is between God and me. As long as I confess it to God, I'm fine."
- "I don't care what the Bible says about..."
- "Well, I'm not nearly as bad as *that* person."
- "That is Old Testament."
- "What I'm doing is normal. *Everyone* struggles with this sin."
- "I don't have to tithe or give to God unless I feel led to."
- "God and I have an understanding."
- "I'm submitted to God; I don't have to submit to any man."
- "When you are as spiritually mature as I am, you will understand."

Dealing With Jezebel: Do's and Don'ts

Do: On a regular basis, ask God to search your heart for things you have hidden from Him and yourself.

Don't: Don't assume that since you've grown spiritually you are immune to falling prey to self-deception (Jezebel spirit).

CHAPTER 6

THE SPIRIT OF JEZEBEL

Jezebel was a person, but a spirit influenced all her evil behavior and characteristics. It's the spirit we want to focus on, not on Jezebel the person (nor any specific person that may be operating in the Jezebel spirit). Throughout the Bible, you will note an extensive list of individuals through whom the spirit of Jezebel was able to operate. When you learn to battle Jezebel spiritually rather than naturally, you will begin to take authority over this spirit in your life.

It is so common to let people become the main focus instead of the true enemy. People are not the enemy. As long as you concentrate on a person, you will never defeat the spirit of Jezebel in your life. In Ephesians 6:12 (NLT), we read, "For we are not fighting against flesh-and-blood enemies, but against evil rulers and authorities of the unseen world, against mighty powers in this dark world, and against evil spirits in the heavenly places."

Let's take a deeper look at the spirit behind the characteristics of Jezebel. Even after a few years of battling the spirit of Jezebel and seeing victory in many areas, I was mistaken about one thing. I thought that if you were mature in spiritual warfare and had defeated the spirit of Jezebel in the past, it would then be safely behind you, never to be seen or heard from again. Oh, how wrong I was.

The second mistake I made was thinking that I ran into Jezebel by chance. I thought they were freak accidents or random occasions when I faced spiritual tests. Nope! I wasn't running into Jezebel—she found me! She is drawn to the prophetic. She is drawn to those that move in the gifts of the Spirit. She engages those who pursue righteousness. She's drawn to them to stop them. My run-ins with

Jezebel were not chance encounters and neither are yours. They are deliberate, premeditated assaults on your life, ministry, and future. These encounters are not going to go away, but we can have victory over this spirit.

Jezebel will always find those who dwell in the presence of God and seek to spread the power of the Holy Spirit around the world. You can't just go to a new church—she'll find you! You can't go to a new city—she'll find you! You can't start a new ministry—she'll show up there, too! If we try to fight people instead of a spirit, we will never be victorious. I can't emphasize this enough; *people are not the enemy*. We need to be aware of this. No matter how much people come against you, or even hurt you, you need to remind yourself continually that there is a spirit behind that person's actions and behavior.

"...PEOPLE ARE NOT THE ENEMY."

Jezebel was possessed by a power older than her human self. Jezebel was the vessel of the spirit that was the source of her evil. Just as God chooses vessels for His glory, Satan chooses vessels for his evil purposes. In Malachi 4:5-6, we read: "'See, I will send you the prophet Elijah before that great and dreadful day of the LORD comes. He will turn the hearts of the fathers to their children, and the hearts of the children to their fathers; or else I will come and strike the land with a curse.'" We are living in the "days of Elijah," the end days when God pours His Spirit out onto His people. Jezebel came against Elijah in his day, and her spirit comes against those of us who carry the spirit and heart of Elijah in this day. So let's see how this spirit has operated through different people throughout the Bible. There are many cases; these are only a few of them.

Eve and Satan

Just a few chapters after the Bible begins, the Jezebel spirit manifests itself through persuasive manipulation. In Genesis 3:1 (NIV), we read: "Now the serpent was more crafty than any of the wild animals the LORD God had made. He said to the woman, 'Did God really say, "You must not eat from any tree in the garden"?'" The word *crafty*, in the Hebrew is translated *Aram* and means *cunning* in this context (usually in a negative sense). The serpent came to separate Adam and Eve from their rightful place of obedience toward God. We see the Jezebel spirit originated with the Devil himself, virtually from the beginning of time. He is the originator of the anti-God, Antichrist spiritual agenda.

David and Saul

An entire book could be written on the correlation between King Saul and the spirit of Jezebel. He was an extremely prideful, overbearing leader. He was the anointed king for only two years, but he reigned as king for forty-two years. In 1 Samuel 13:1 (NIV1984), we read, "Saul was thirty years old when he became king, and he reigned over Israel forty-two years." This means Saul had a forty year reign of *pride*! He ruled over Israel with a flesh-ruled heart for forty years. While ruling in self-deceived pride, he became a tyrannical leader! He desired the approval of man over God. In 1 Samuel 15:24 (NLT), we read: "Then Saul admitted to Samuel, 'Yes, I have sinned. I have disobeyed your instructions and the LORD's command, for I was afraid of the people and did what they demanded.'" He said this within the context of a climactic event in his rule when he usurped biblical authority and offered unauthorized sacrifices.

> Some Hebrews even crossed the Jordan to the land of Gad and Gilead.

Saul remained at Gilgal, and all the troops with him were quaking with fear. He waited seven days, the time set by Samuel; but Samuel did not come to Gilgal, and Saul's men began to scatter. So he said, "Bring me the burnt offering and the fellowship offerings." And Saul offered up the burnt offering. Just as he finished making the offering, Samuel arrived, and Saul went out to greet him. "What have you done?" asked Samuel. Saul replied, "When I saw that the men were scattering, and that you did not come at the set time, and that the Philistines were assembling at Micmash, I thought, 'Now the Philistines will come down against me at Gilgal, and I have not sought the LORD's favor.' So I felt compelled to offer the burnt offering." "You acted foolishly," Samuel said. "You have not kept the command the LORD your God gave you; if you had, he would have established your kingdom over Israel for all time. (1 Samuel 13:7-13, NIV1984)

Saul was extremely jealous! In 1 Samuel 18:9, we read, "And from that time on Saul kept a jealous eye on David." Through his rebellion and disobedience, the spirit of Jezebel grew stronger in Saul. In 1 Samuel 15:23 (NLT), Samuel pronounces God's judgment on Saul: "Rebellion is as sinful as witchcraft, and stubbornness as bad as worshiping idols. So because you have rejected the command of the LORD, he has rejected you as king." It got to the point where the man-made king was so far gone that he resorted to occultism, participating in séances, using mediums to channel dead spirits! First Samuel 28:6-8 (NIV) says of Saul: "He inquired of the LORD, but the LORD did not answer him by dreams or Urim or prophets. Saul then said to his attendants, 'Find me a woman who is a medium, so I may go and inquire of her.' 'There is one in Endor,' they said. So Saul disguised himself, putting on other clothes, and at night he and two men went to the woman. 'Consult a spirit for me,' he said, 'and bring up for me the one I name.'"

The spirit of Jezebel became so strong in Saul's life that he resorted to attempt to preemptively murder the one who was truly anointed king—David! In 1 Samuel 19:9-11 (NIV), we read: "But an evil spirit from the LORD came upon Saul as he was sitting in his house with his spear in his hand. While David was playing the harp, Saul tried to pin him to the wall with his spear, but David eluded him as Saul drove the spear into the wall. That night David made good his escape. Saul sent men to David's house to watch it and to kill him in the morning. But Michal, David's wife, warned him, 'If you don't run for your life tonight, tomorrow you'll be killed.'"

Samson and Delilah

We see the seduction and manipulation of the spirit of Jezebel in the relationship between Samson and Delilah. Samson was an anointed leader with the Spirit of God on his life. Delilah was a vehicle for the spirit of Jezebel to stop him from fulfilling the call of God on his life. The relationship was birthed in the flesh. Notice that word, "flesh," keeps coming up.

Delilah's name (dĭ lĭ'lə) comes from the Arabic *dallatum* and means, *flirt*. We don't know if she was a Philistine or an Israelite. It would make sense if she was a Philistine, for their God was Baal. Either way, she manipulated Samson for money, a source of power and motivation for Jezebel. She used sex and pouting as tools of manipulation on Samson. In Judges 16:15-16 (NLT), we read: "Then Delilah pouted, 'How can you tell me, "I love you," when you don't share your secrets with me? You've made fun of me three times now, and you still haven't told me what makes you so strong!' She tormented him with her nagging day after day until he was sick to death of it." Delilah wore Samson down until he finally gave up and gave in to the spirit of Jezebel. Samson lost his will and by giving it to Jezebel, consequently, he also lost his strength. When you give in to the spirit of Jezebel, as Samson and many others have done, you will lose your will and strength to fight!

Mordecai and Haman

In the Book of Esther, a man named Haman wanted to annihilate the Children of Israel due to his jealousy of an Israelite named Mordecai. He wanted them all dead. He devised a wicked plan to trick the king into signing a law that insured all Jews would be put to death. Haman's deceit was successful and the malicious law was passed! Haman usurped the king's authority through deception. In Esther 3:10-11 (NLT), we read: "The king agreed, confirming his decision by removing his signet ring from his finger and giving it to Haman son of Hammedatha the Agagite, the enemy of the Jews. The king said, 'The money and the people are both yours to do with as you see fit.'" The spirit of Jezebel was in full force. Haman had complete power to put God's people to death.

God used Mordecai to give Esther the wisdom to confront Haman. Through prayer and fasting, they warred against the Jezebel spirit. Esther 4:15-16 (NLT) recounts: "Then Esther sent this reply to Mordecai: 'Go and gather together all the Jews of Susa and fast for me. Do not eat or drink for three days, night or day. My maids and I will do the same. And then, though it is against the law, I will go in to see the king. If I must die, I must die.'"

Esther exposed Haman's plan to the king and saved her people. After Haman was exposed, he demonstrated even more characteristics of Jezebel: unrestrained emotions, childish outbursts, improper sexual and physical acts, and more. In Esther 7:8 (NIV), we read: "Just as the king returned from the palace garden to the banquet hall, Haman was falling on the couch where Esther was reclining. The king exclaimed, 'Will he even molest the queen while she is with me in the house?' As soon as the word left the king's mouth, they covered Haman's face." Haman had behaved so forcefully and with such a lack of restraint that the king accused him of attempting to molest Queen Esther!

It is symbolic that they covered Haman's face. Jezebel used her "painted eyes" to intimidate and the king's servants covered Haman's face to end his oppressive intimidation.

The Church of Thyatira exhibited Jezebel inspired, unrestrained behavior that eerily mirrored Haman's. Jesus addressed this Jezebel spirit in Revelation 2:22 (NIV), "So I will cast her on a bed of suffering, and I will make those who commit adultery with her suffer intensely, unless they repent of her ways."

Haman died the same type of death as Jezebel. They were both killed "from the high place.": Jezebel was thrown down from her tower and Haman was hung on high gallows he had made for Mordecai. Esther 7:9—10 (NIV) recounts: "A gallows seventy-five feet high stands by Haman's house. He had it made for Mordecai, who spoke up to help the king. The king said, 'Hang him on it!' So they hanged Haman on the gallows he had prepared for Mordecai. Then the king's fury subsided." The prayer and wisdom of Queen Esther and Mordecai saved God's people from death and destruction by the spirit of Jezebel working through Haman.

Nehemiah and Sanballat

God gave Nehemiah a specific assignment. He was led by the Spirit of God to rebuild the walls of Jerusalem. Nehemiah had received unmerited favor from the king as well as aid for his project. In Nehemiah 4:1-2 (NIV), we read: "When Sanballat heard that we were rebuilding the wall, he became angry and was greatly incensed. He ridiculed the Jews, and in the presence of his associates and the army of Samaria, he said, 'What are those feeble Jews doing? Will they restore their wall? Will they offer sacrifices? Will they finish in a day? Can they bring the stones back to life from those heaps of rubble— burned as they are?'" Sanballat used fear and intimidation and did everything else he could to come against Nehemiah and distract him from doing the will of God. In Nehemiah 4:8 (NIV), we read, "They all plotted together to come and fight against Jerusalem and stir up trouble against it." Nehemiah was unfazed and determined to do the Lord's work.

Like Jezebel, Sanballat resorted to intimidation. He sent five messengers with letters to try to distract and stop Nehemiah. In

Nehemiah 6:5 (NIV), he writes, "Then, the fifth time, Sanballat sent his aide to me with the same message, and in his hand was an unsealed letter." Every time Nehemiah received a letter from Sanballat, he discerned the spirit of fear behind the person of Sanballat and responded in faith. In Nehemiah 6:9 (NIV), he writes, "They were all trying to frighten us, thinking, 'Their hands will get too weak for the work, and it will not be completed.' But I prayed, 'Now strengthen my hands.'" This is a perfect prayer for anyone to pray when facing spiritual opposition from the Jezebel spirit: "Lord, strengthen my hands (strengthen me)!"

John the Baptist and Herodias

Of all the men of God in the Bible, John the Baptist most resembles Elijah in both his spirit and ministry. An angel appeared to his parents, prophesying his coming and that John would walk in the same spirit Elijah had. In Luke 1:17 (NIV), we read: "And he will go on before the Lord, in the spirit and power of Elijah, to turn the hearts of the parents to their children and the disobedient to the wisdom of the righteous—to make ready a people prepared for the Lord."

Both John the Baptist and the spirit of Elijah represent the Holy Spirit. They represent the Spirit that prepares the coming of the Lord. It is no surprise that the spirit of Jezebel would find and come against John the Baptist, a man who walked in the power and spirit of Elijah. Jezebel operated through a queen named Herodias. She hated John with a passion because he confronted her sin when other righteous men were too intimidated by her to do so. In Matthew 14:3-5 (NIV), we read: "Now Herod had arrested John and bound him and put him in prison because of Herodias, his brother Philip's wife, for John had been saying to him: 'It is not lawful for you to have her.' Herod wanted to kill John, but he was afraid of the people, because they considered John a prophet."

Herod held a great feast at which Herodias's daughter danced before him (seductively, most likely). The king was so pleased by her demonic dance that he told the girl he wanted to give her a special gift—her choice. Jezebel, at work in Herodias, saw her opportunity. In Matthew 14:8-11 (NIV), we read: "Prompted by her mother, she said, 'Give me here on a platter the head of John the Baptist.' The king was distressed, but because of his oaths and his dinner guests, he ordered that her request be granted and had John beheaded in the prison. His head was brought in on a platter and given to the girl, who carried it to her mother." More than anything, Herodias wanted John the Baptist dead, so obsessed was she with her hatred of him. John the Baptist's earthly life was ended that day, but he had already accomplished his life's assignment. He had prepared the way of the Lord Jesus!

Jesus and the Pharisees

If Jezebel comes against the move of the Spirit of God, it is no surprise when she unleashes her greatest evil by coming against the Spirit of God Himself in Jesus. (Jesus Christ was all man and all God.) Jezebel channeled herself through religious leaders to war against the very Spirit of the living God. From the beginning of Jesus's ministry, the Pharisees (church leaders) vehemently opposed everything He did and everything He said. In Luke 4:14-15 (NIV), we read: "Jesus returned to Galilee in the power of the Spirit, and news about him spread through the whole countryside. He taught in their synagogues, and everyone praised him." Jesus, God in the flesh, was filled with the Spirit of God. When people saw this they were amazed. The people and the crowds began to look to Jesus and not the religious leaders.

When Jesus began to walk, talk, and minister in his God-given authority, Jezebel set to work doing what she does best. She always starts with pride, just as Satan does. Satan begins everything in pride; it's his first nature. Jezebel must be the center of attention. Everything she does is to be seen.

Jesus knew the Pharisees and religious leaders were operating with these selfish motives, and He didn't hold back on calling them out!

"When you pray, don't be like the hypocrites who love to pray publicly on street corners and in the synagogues where everyone can see them. I tell you the truth, that is all the reward they will ever get. But when you pray, go away by yourself, shut the door behind you, and pray to your Father in private. Then your Father, who sees everything, will reward you. When you pray, don't babble on and on as people of other religions do. They think their prayers are answered merely by repeating their words again and again. Don't be like them, for your Father knows exactly what you need even before you ask him!" (Matthew 6:5-8, NLT)

Jesus told the world not to be like the religious leaders. The religious, Jezebel leaders hated Jesus for this. But the reason they might have hated Him most was the money they lost after people began sowing into Jesus's ministry! In Luke 8:1-3 (NIV), we read: "After this, Jesus traveled about from one town and village to another, proclaiming the good news of the kingdom of God. The Twelve were with him, and also some women who had been cured of evil spirits and diseases: Mary (called Magdalene) from whom seven demons had come out; Joanna the wife of Chuza, the manager of Herod's household; Susanna; and many others. These women were helping to support them out of their own means." This might have been the straw that broke the camel's back. Wealthy, affluent people began to give to the ministry of Jesus and not to them. In spite of all their opposition and hatred, Jesus never allowed the Jezebel spirit to hinder Him!

Nevertheless, Jezebel continued her scripted routine and raised the stakes. In Luke 4:28-30 (NLT), we read: " When they heard this, the people in the synagogue were furious. Jumping up, they mobbed him and forced him to the edge of the hill on which the town was built. They intended to push him over the cliff, but he passed right through the crowd and went on his way." This is such an insightful scripture. Jezebel tried to kill Jesus before the cross, yet Jesus transcended the crowd. Jezebel couldn't kill Him because Jesus was not to be murdered before the cross. He was to be offered up as a living sacrifice. Jesus shows us how to defeat and conquer the spirit of Jezebel.

The spirit of Jezebel will operate through people who have resisted the Holy Spirit and given in to her. We have looked at numerous examples of this spirit operating through men and women throughout the Bible. In all these cases, it always comes back to a spirit, never a person. We must be aware of this and learn to fight the spirit of Jezebel and deal with people. If we're fighting people, we have already lost!

"IF WE'RE FIGHTING PEOPLE, WE HAVE ALREADY LOST!"

Dealing With Jezebel: Do's and Don'ts

Do: Confront the person but spiritually war against the spirit of Jezebel.

Don't: Don't allow any single person to take your focus off the spirit of Jezebel that is in operation.

CHAPTER 7

THE FAMILY TREE

In this chapter, we will take a deeper look into Jezebel's immediate family. The Jezebel spirit wreaks havoc on the family and church body. This spirit operates generationally and, without a strong spiritual leader to stop it, runs free to torment and ruin relationships. More times than not, the Jezebel spirit is enabled and empowered by a close family dynamic or insecure leadership that appears to be spiritually healthy, but in actuality is corrupt to the core. Jezebel's enabled behavior has a devastating effect on families and churches.

It's important to reflect on how you were raised. Many Christians do not regularly practice stopping to ask themselves, "Why do I think the way I do?" or more importantly, "Do my beliefs line up with the Word of God?" Far too many who claim to be Christians say what they want, do what they want, vote however they want, and respond however they want with no regard to what the Bible says. It's much easier to say, "I did this because...my family is Italian," "...I'm hot-tempered—I'm Irish," or "...this is just the way I am" and so on, thus justifying our decisions and behavior. Far too many of us make excuses for our decisions and behavior rather than changing them or challenging them with the Word of God.

In fact, family dynamics are so strong and influential in forming our beliefs and behaviors, they often trump the teachings of the Bible in our hearts. Jesus knew this. That's why He made this point in Matthew 12:48-50 (NLT): "Jesus asked, 'Who is my mother? Who are my brothers?' Then he pointed to his disciples and said, 'Look, these are my mother and brothers. Anyone who does the will of my Father in heaven is my brother and sister and mother!'" What makes this scripture so interesting is that Jesus had a good relationship with His family. So why did He say it? To show us that our relationship with God needs to be *greater* than our relationships with even our closest family members.

THE FAMILY TREE

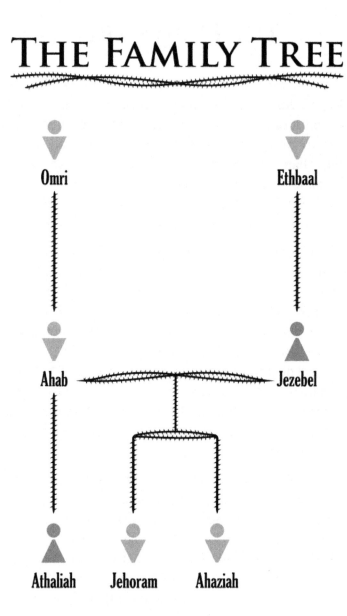

Jezebel was raised by her father, a priest of Baal. He trained her to operate in the ways she did. He taught her manipulation, fear tactics, how to threaten, and the art of intimidation. She learned by watching him! The spirit of Jezebel is generational because children learn by watching their parents. They watch how divorced parents try to one-up each other to be the "favorite" parent. They watch and listen as their parents leave a Sunday morning service talking down the pastor and the church. They hear comments like, "The only thing the church wants is our money." They are discipled into pride with comments like, "No one talks to me like that!" Children watch single parents date ungodly people and cohabitate in unholy lifestyles. Then on Sunday, children watch their parents go to church as if all is well. Children will mimic the behavior of Jezebel step by step until they fall more fully under her influence. After youth pastoring for over ten years, I've seen many parents throw their hands up in frustration and say: "I don't know why my child is acting like this. It must be just a normal teenage thing." No! In many cases, they have learned their negative behavior from their parents.

"THE SPIRIT OF JEZEBEL IS GENERATIONAL BECAUSE CHILDREN LEARN BY WATCHING THEIR PARENTS."

No Wonder He Acted Like That

A mother of one of the young people in my youth ministry stopped me after church one day and said she really needed to talk with me. So, we set up a time to meet later that week. She was a single mom, so I brought my wife along to the meeting for accountability. She opened up by telling us how great we were and how honored she was that we would take the time to meet with her. I thanked her and she proceeded to share how her son wasn't doing very well in school and being very disrespectful at home. These were relatively normal things I heard from parents from time to time.

In the middle of her story, the woman took an abrasive turn and began telling us how the pastors at her last church would not meet with her, and how greatly it upset her that they ignored many of her requests.

She said, "They told me that it would be a month before they could meet with me. Can you believe that?"

"You know, some pastors are very busy, perhaps it was just a hectic month," I said.

She didn't appear to be convinced. I asked her how long she had attended her last church and she said it had been a few years. Meanwhile, I was detecting that she was not emotionally stable. I knew I needed to choose all my words very carefully. I also knew the worst way to build a relationship with a pastor was to start off by talking badly about one's last pastor. And I knew that if she talked like this about her last pastor in our first conversation, it wouldn't be long before she was talking this way about me!

I finally told her the best thing she could do was write her last pastor a letter, thanking him for everything he did for her son—and give him some kind of small gift. She listened to me and said she would. We prayed together and ended the meeting.

Later that week, I got a call from the church secretary with a message to call this woman ASAP. I called her and she told me her son had lost it! He was throwing dishes and kicking holes in the wall. She was at work and her son was home alone, so I went over and picked him up. When I asked him why he had done these things, he said very honestly, "I really don't know." I believed him. He didn't know why he was acting out like he had and he didn't have a real reason.

The next day, my wife and I met with the woman again. I asked her if she had written the letter to her last pastor as I had suggested. She said, "Well, kind of." I stayed quiet and let her explain. "I started writing it like you said, and then all of a sudden I got so mad at him that I started writing about how disappointed I was with the way he had shown he didn't care about my son!" She had done the absolute opposite of what I told her to do. It is no wonder her son demonstrated rebellion with outbursts and fits of rage. His mother was discipling him in rebellion. Not even four months later, this woman was back at her old church, saying bad things about me.

We must teach our children righteousness. We must live holy lives before them, giving them a righteous example to follow. Tell your children when you are wrong. Repent to them when you make mistakes. We need to take opportunities to display genuine humility and must not allow the spirit of Jezebel to continue in our families.

"The spirit of Jezebel can't take power without an Ahab."

Jezebel married a man named Ahab. The spirit of Jezebel can't take power without an Ahab. Ahab was an enabler who allowed Jezebel to live her life without submitting to any authority. He allowed her to behave in ways that were way out of order. He allowed it because it benefitted him. Jezebel fought Ahab's battles and did the dirty work so he could be the good guy.

Some time later there was an incident involving a vineyard belonging to Naboth the Jezreelite. The vineyard was in Jezreel, close to the palace of Ahab king of Samaria. Ahab said to Naboth, "Let me have your vineyard to use for a vegetable garden, since it is close to my palace. In exchange I will give you a better vineyard or, if you prefer, I will pay you whatever it is worth." But Naboth replied, "The LORD forbid that I should give you the inheritance of my fathers." So Ahab went home, sullen and angry because Naboth the Jezreelite had said, "I will not give you the inheritance of my fathers." He lay on his bed sulking and refused to eat. His wife Jezebel came in and asked him, "Why are you so sullen? Why won't you eat?" He answered her, "Because I said to Naboth the Jezreelite, 'Sell me your vineyard; or if you prefer, I will give you another vineyard in its place.' But he said, 'I will not give you my vineyard.'" Jezebel his wife said, "Is this how you act as king over Israel? Get up and eat! Cheer up. I'll get you the vineyard of Naboth the Jezreelite." (1 Kings 21:1-7, NIV1984)

Ahab knew that Jezebel was going to take the vineyard wrongfully, but he didn't want to know the details. After all, if he didn't know the details, he assumed he wasn't responsible for the outcome!

A Perverse Prophecy

Steve was a minister who flowed in the Holy Spirit. As he ministered one Sunday night, the Holy Spirit was moving powerfully. People were all over the altar area, crying out to the Lord. Steve was still on the stage praying as the band ministered over the people. Suddenly, the associate pastor approached him. He leaned into Steve's ear and said, "I had a prophetic dream about you this week and I've been hesitant to share it with you. I feel as if I'm supposed to share it with you tonight." (Notice that he tells Steve it's prophetic rather than letting God tell Steve this, or allowing him to discern this himself.) He began to share: "We were all at a staff pool party. Everyone was in and around the pool. You came out with a Speedo on. Then you took off your Speedo in front of all of us and jumped into the pool." Steve wondered where in the world this was headed. Then the associate pastor said to him, "Steve, when you took off your Speedo I noticed you were uncircumcised. I believe there are areas in your life God wants you to circumcise."

WHAT? Steve couldn't believe what he had just heard. It was the most foul, revolting thing he had ever heard uttered in the name of the Lord. Steve just turned and walked away. He knew this "prophetic word" wasn't going to fly. He also knew this was too big of a deal to just let go by. This high-ranking associate pastor had just delivered a vile word to him. Steve felt as if the man had spoken perversion over him.

This "word" really bothered Steve and he just couldn't shake it off. When he got home that night, he immediately shared with his wife what had happened and they prayed together, rebuking the demonic word. After getting wise counsel from his mentors, he decided to go to the lead pastor of the church to tell him what happened without telling him who said it, except to tell him it was a staff member. Steve's strategy was that he would allow his pastor to hear it and condemn it. Then when the pastor asked who said it, he would tell him. This way it wouldn't look like Steve was trying to attack the associate pastor.

The next day, Steve told the lead pastor exactly what had happened. The pastor instantly told Steve he knew the word wasn't from God. Then Steve sat there, waiting for the pastor to ask who had spoken the word, thinking surely he would want to know—especially since a member of his staff had given the word. Steve just kept waiting and waiting. The lead pastor never asked. He didn't want to know. Why would he not want to know and deal with someone on his staff who had said this? It is simply this: Ahabs are enablers to the Jezebel spirit.

"THOSE WHO SERVE JEZEBEL DIE FIRST!"

I used to think that Ahab was a casualty of Jezebel's war. No. Ahab is the arms dealer that enables her wars. If men of God would take their rightful authority in their churches, workplaces, and families, and confront Jezebel, her tyranny would come to an end. *Those who serve Jezebel die first!* It might appear that they are safe behind Jezebel, but she always makes sure others fall before her. Consider this account of Ahab's demise:

> So the king of Israel and Jehoshaphat king of Judah went up to Ramoth Gilead. The king of Israel said to Jehoshaphat, "I will enter the battle in disguise, but you wear your royal robes." So the king of Israel disguised himself and went into battle....But someone drew his bow at random and hit the king of Israel between the sections of his armor. The king told his chariot driver, "Wheel around and get me out of the fighting. I've been wounded." All day long the battle raged, and the king was propped up in his chariot facing the Arameans. The blood from his wound ran onto the floor of the chariot, and that evening he died. As the sun was setting, a cry spread through the army: "Every man to his town; everyone to his land!" So the king died and was brought to Samaria, and they buried him there. They washed the chariot at a pool in Samaria (where the prostitutes bathed), and the dogs licked up his blood, as the word of the LORD had declared. (1 Kings 22:29-38, NIV)

Ahab and Jezebel had two sons, Ahaziah and Jehoram (also referred to as Joram), and a daughter, Athaliah. Jezebel was so selfish, she raised her children in a manner that practically insured they would suffer the same fate she did. She raised them to resist God with a reckless abandon, to rebel against God at any price. (And they would pay that price.) None of them were successful leaders, their empires didn't last long, and all of them experienced a painful death.

Ahaziah son of Ahab began to rule over Israel in the seventeenth year of King Jehoshaphat's reign in Judah. He reigned in Samaria two years. But he did what was evil in the LORD's sight, following the example of his father and mother and the example of Jeroboam son of Nebat, who had led Israel to sin. He served Baal and worshiped him, provoking the anger of the LORD, the God of Israel, just as his father had done. (1 Kings 22:51-53, NLT)

And Elijah said to the king, "This is what the LORD says: Why did you send messengers to Baal-zebub, the god of Ekron, to ask whether you will recover? Is there no God in Israel to answer your question? Therefore, because you have done this, you will never leave the bed you are lying on; you will surely die." So Ahaziah died, just as the LORD had promised through Elijah. (2 Kings 1:16-17, NLT)

Ahab's son Joram* began to rule over Israel in the eighteenth year of King Jehoshaphat's reign in Judah. He reigned in Samaria twelve years. He did what was evil in the LORD's sight, but not to the same extent as his father and mother. He at least tore down the sacred pillar of Baal that his father had set up. (2 Kings 3:1-2)

Then Jehoiada the priest ordered the commanders who were in charge of the troops, "Take her (Athaliah) to the soldiers in front of the Temple,* and kill anyone who tries to rescue her." For the priest had said, "She must not be killed in the Temple of the LORD." So they seized her and led her out to the gate where horses enter the palace grounds, and she was killed there. (2 Kings 11:15-16, NLT)

"JEZEBEL RUNS THE FAMILY AND JEZEBEL RUINS THE FAMILY."

Jezebel runs the family and Jezebel ruins the family. This spirit will continue generationally until someone in the family line confronts it and breaks the strongholds!

Dealing With Jezebels: Do's and Don'ts

Do: Admit to your family, children, and friends when you are wrong. Imitate the humility of Jesus.

Don't: Don't allow Jezebel around your children or to be divisive in your marriage.

CHAPTER 8

SPIRITUAL ABORTION

The end result of a fully mature Jezebel spirit is death. The original Jezebel brought death to God's prophets and to her own family. The spirit of Jezebel brings a spirit of death to natural families and spiritual families. It destroys the fruit of churches. It aborts the relationship between pastors and their spiritual children and destroys the future of churches and the legacy that God intends for His people.

Abortion has been at the center of the moral decline of America, since 1973's *Roe v. Wade*, which legalized it. Since then, over fifty million babies have been aborted in the US. This is a staggering statistic and the greatest sign that America has developed into an incredibly selfish, anti-God nation. We wonder why our nation is spiraling into economic recession. I think we have to ask...why *shouldn't* it? Then we have to ask ourselves: Can God bless this nation that has murdered its own? Can God bless those who have sacrificed their children out of their own selfishness? I do not believe the answer to these questions is yes!

Queen Jezebel worshiped the false god, Baal, which included child sacrifice. This included the murder of the unborn (abortion) and newborn babies. When female prostitutes of Baal were impregnated during religious "services," they would sacrifice these conceived children to Baal.

There is no inheritance for an aborted child. I believe that the spirit of Jezebel's greatest attack on any church is on its legacy. It's a spiritual abortion to destroy the spiritual inheritance that is to be passed down from generation to generation. In the story of Naboth's vineyard, we find revelation of this attack on spiritual inheritance.

Naboth refused to give to Ahab what he valued most, his inheritance (1 Kings 21).

Throughout the Bible, the vineyard symbolizes the family. Naboth would not give his legacy to Jezebel. He would not surrender his spiritual family to her cause. I can't tell you how many people I have talked to that have told me story after story of relationships they lost with family members, pastors, spiritual parents, and friends because Jezebel influenced their spiritual parents to commit spiritual abortion. These relationships were sacrificed on the altar of Baal and the result was broken people, destroyed lives, empty churches, and lost legacies. *Jezebel will put her religion (ministry) before her children.* She will put her church before the spiritual children in it. She will put her hunger for power, control, and pride before any spiritual son or daughter.

"JEZEBEL WILL PUT HER RELIGION (MINISTRY) BEFORE HER CHILDREN."

You're Not A Son

Henry had faithfully served his pastor for over ten years in a church he had attended since he was in the fifth grade. His pastor had conducted his wedding and was present when his children were born. After serving as an assistant to his pastor for years, he was promoted to be the head of operations, overseeing the entire ministry. Over the years, Henry served his pastor and the church faithfully, through thick and thin.

Henry's natural father wasn't involved and his father-in-law had died suddenly, leaving Henry and his wife truly fatherless. His pastor of seventeen years had been his only spiritual father, and now he was the only "father" Henry had left.

Sadly, the spirit of Jezebel made its way into the church and began to influence the pastor's decision-making. He began making erratic choices, changing directions from one thing to the next and every time telling the church that God was taking them into a new season and that they were now going in a new direction. Finally, one of Henry's closest friends was asked to leave the church after standing up to the pastor on a few issues. Henry had known this friend for over twelve years.

Henry's pastor told him he had to cut off relationship with this friend if he intended to remain loyal to the church, but Henry was unwilling to cut off the relationship with his childhood friend. He knew it wasn't the right, biblical thing to do. Henry's pastor caught wind of the fact that he was still talking to and spending time with his friend.

After a Wednesday night service, the pastor confronted Henry about it. He began to question him, angrily demanding to know if it was true. Not wanting to upset his pastor, Henry reluctantly admitted he was indeed still friends with the man. His pastor lost it and exploded in a scathing tirade, ending it with this: "Well I guess this settles it! From now on, you are not a spiritual son! Nope, you're just an employee! My sons protect me, Henry. My sons obey me, Henry. Sons honor their spiritual fathers, so you're obviously not a son! You're just an employee and you will be treated like an employee from now on!" With that, Henry's pastor and spiritual father got in his car and drove away.

Henry went home to his wife. With tears in his eyes and a cracking voice, he told her the details of the story. "He said I'm not a son!" Henry said over and over. The spirit of Jezebel operating through his pastor knew what button to push. This spirit knew how to crush Henry and bring him to his knees. With everything in him, Henry wanted to be a good son. When his pastor couldn't control his spiritual son, he committed spiritual abortion and killed the relationship.

Within two weeks, Henry no longer worked at the church. He was told it would be best if he and his family did not attend the church any longer. His pastor went from being the father figure that stood at the bedside in the hospital as his children were born to a man that avoided Henry in the mall, pretending he didn't see him. His now former pastor treated Henry as if he were dead to him...because he was. His pastor had spiritually aborted him!

Jezebel doesn't know how to raise spiritual sons and daughters. This is why she aborts them. She is the queen of dysfunction. I've been in too many greenrooms before church services where I witnessed pastors verbally breaking down and belittling those who served them, only to then turn to me and smirk, "A little discipline is good for them." I agree, a little discipline is good for everyone, but abuse is good for no one! Jezebel doesn't know how to parent. She doesn't know how to raise spiritual children. *That's why she has none.*

"JEZEBEL DOESN'T KNOW HOW TO RAISE SPIRITUAL SONS AND DAUGHTERS. THIS IS WHY SHE ABORTS THEM."

I've noticed this trend in some large ministries around the country—those with which everyone seems to be impressed. Sadly, many ministers aspire to be like them. Before you get too impressed with any minister, ask yourself this question: Where are their spiritual sons and daughters? In fact, take the question even further: Where are their natural sons and daughters? Many of the children of these leaders do not serve God. These ministers may have large ministries, but very little spiritual fruit. Why? Jezebel doesn't want spiritual children, she wants slaves to serve her!

"Jezebel doesn't want spiritual children, she wants slaves to serve her!"

King Saul gave us many examples of Jezebel characteristics and behavior. Saul flew into a rage when David transitioned from being a servant to being a son. David began his ministry by serving Saul. In 1 Samuel 16:21 (NLT), we read: "So David went to Saul and began serving him. Saul loved David very much, and David became his armor bearer." When David was promoted, the insecurity in Saul wouldn't allow the sonship developing in David to grow. Saul committed spiritual abortion on David. In 1 Samuel 19:9–10 (NLT), we read: "But one day when Saul was sitting at home, with spear in hand, the tormenting spirit from the LORD suddenly came upon him again. As David played his harp, Saul hurled his spear at David. But David dodged out of the way, and leaving the spear stuck in the wall, he fled and escaped into the night."

Many leaders do the same thing. When their spiritual sons rise up, they are intimidated, become jealous of them and sabotage the relationship by spiritually aborting them. Despite Saul being a bad father, David was a good son—and even Saul knew it.

When David had finished speaking, Saul called back, "Is that really you, my son David?" Then he began to cry. And he said to David, "You are a better man than I am, for you have repaid me good for evil. Yes, you have been amazingly kind to me today, for when the LORD put me in a place where you could have killed me, you didn't do it. Who else would let his enemy get away when he had him in his power? May the LORD reward you well for the kindness you have shown me today. And now I realize that you are surely going to be king, and that the kingdom of Israel will flourish under your rule." (1 Samuel 24:16-20, NLT)

If God would have taken Elijah's life as he asked (1 Kings 19:4), there would have been no Elisha, his spiritual son. There would have been no school of the prophets. There would have been no legacy. God is the God of legacy. God gave Elijah the heart of a father and did not send him to produce a large church, nor an international ministry, but a spiritual son.

God used the prophet Malachi to prophesy the return of the spirit of Elijah that would reconnect the hearts of spiritual children to their spiritual parents and break the stronghold of the spirit of abortion that is destroying families and churches. In Malachi 4:5-6, we read: "Behold, I send you Elijah the prophet before the coming of the day of the Lord, great and terrible day. And he shall turn the hearts of the fathers to the children and the hearts of children to their fathers, lest I come and smite the earth with a curse." This is the "spirit of adoption." In Romans 8:15-17 (NLT), we read: "So you have not received a spirit that makes you fearful slaves. Instead, you received God's Spirit when he adopted you as his own children. Now we call him, 'Abba, Father.' For his Spirit joins with our spirit to affirm that we are God's children. And since we are his children, we are his heirs." So powerful!

Perhaps you have been extremely hurt by a spiritual father or mother, natural parent, or leader. You may have been devastated to the point of walking away from church or even God. This is the enemy's plan. Know this: Even if you have been rejected by a parent, pastor, or spiritual mentor, *you are not an orphan!* You cannot be an orphan because to be an orphan means you were somehow abandoned by both your parents. That's impossible because Jesus said He will never leave you nor forsake you (Hebrews 13:5). God has not rejected you. You can reject Him, but God will never leave you. You are not alone!

We are heirs of Christ, adopted by Him (Ephesians 1:5). Even if a spiritual parent aborted you, the Spirit of Christ has adopted you! You are not dead but alive in Christ! The heart of the Father is to adopt His children, to save them from a spiritual abortion and give them a spiritual legacy!

Dealing With Jezebel: Do's and Don'ts

Do: Find a righteous man or woman of God who wants to be a spiritual father or mother. Learn from him or her.

Don't: Don't become bitter and give up on biblical discipleship, mentorship, and sonship.

CHAPTER 9

THE SENSUAL SIDE OF JEZEBEL

Let's dive into the sexuality that is at the center of the spirit of Jezebel. More than sex, her attempt to liberate sexuality is only a ploy to mock God. She hides perversion in media, art, tolerance, equality, and in many other ways. Her religion is sex—sex with a purpose. It is sex that defiles individuals that were made in the image of God, and it is meant to mock their creator. Jezebel is bold in her sexual exploits and her agenda is prevailing. Through confusion, this Antichrist spirit is designed to damage people in order to hurt God.

The spirit of Jezebel runs parallel with the great "whore of Babylon" described in Revelation 17:1-2 (NLT), we read: "One of the seven angels who had poured out the seven bowls came over and spoke to me. 'Come with me,' he said, 'and I will show you the judgment that is going to come on the great prostitute, who rules over many waters. The kings of the world have committed adultery with her, and the people who belong to this world have been made drunk by the wine of her immorality.'" Jezebel has a dominant sexual nature. Everything she does has the power of seduction within it, and women seduce men. If a man falls prey to her seduction, she controls him. Proverbs warns us of this seduction and its result.

I saw some naive young men,
and one in particular who lacked common sense.
He was crossing the street near the house of an immoral woman,
strolling down the path by her house.
It was at twilight, in the evening,
as deep darkness fell.

The woman approached him,
seductively dressed and sly of heart.
She was the brash, rebellious type,
never content to stay at home.
She is often in the streets and markets,
soliciting at every corner.
She threw her arms around him and kissed him,
and with a brazen look she said,
"I've just made my peace offerings
and fulfilled my vows.
You're the one I was looking for!
I came out to find you, and here you are!
My bed is spread with beautiful blankets,
with colored sheets of Egyptian linen.
I've perfumed my bed
with myrrh, aloes, and cinnamon.
Come, let's drink our fill of love until morning.
Let's enjoy each other's caresses,
for my husband is not home.
He's away on a long trip.
He has taken a wallet full of money with him
and won't return until later this month."

So she seduced him with her pretty speech
and enticed him with her flattery.
He followed her at once,
like an ox going to the slaughter.
He was like a stag caught in a trap,
awaiting the arrow that would pierce its heart.
He was like a bird flying into a snare,
little knowing it would cost him his life. (Proverbs 7:7-23, NLT)

Did you read this passage carefully? Notice that the seductress looked for the naive man (self-deceived), and when he gives in to her, it cost him everything. *Perversion will cost you everything!* My father used to tell me, "Son, the immoral man will lose his health, wealth, and family." That has stuck with me my entire life. And I have seen it proven true over the years. Many times, adultery destroys families completely. Even when it does not, it can so damage a family that it takes years for members to regain trust. Pornography prepares individuals to destroy their marriages. All of this destruction is linked to sexual immorality.

"PERVERSION WILL COST YOU EVERYTHING!"

Sometimes, I've asked couples, "What would you do if you were out on a date and someone came up and just started stripping off their clothes in front of your husband or wife?" Taken aback by the question, most people come up with an answer like, "We would leave right away." Feistier ones mention inflicting pain on the one who would do such an obscene thing. Then I say, "Well, that's what happens when you sit through a movie with nudity or sex scenes." *We actually pay money for Jezebel to seduce us!* Immorality is celebrated outwardly in this world and secretly within the Church. Satan is using our lack of self-control to destroy us. Instead of running from

"SATAN IS USING OUR LACK OF SELF-CONTROL TO DESTROY US."

sexual sin, we are running to it. In 1 Corinthians 6:18-20 (NLT), we are told: "Run from sexual sin! No other sin so clearly affects the body as this one does. For sexual immorality is a sin against your own body. Don't you realize that your body is the temple of the Holy Spirit, who lives in you and was given to you by God? You do not belong to yourself, for God bought you with a high price. So you must honor God with your body."

Seduction is often gradual and happens over time. Rarely does someone wake up and say to themselves, "I want to go defile my body and sin sexually today!" It typically starts with a little bit of seduction that leads to one little compromise and another until it becomes a lifestyle of indulgence. Satan knows how destructive sexual sin is to God's children. Look at this verse from a Bible account of a prophet named Balaam: "They were the ones who followed Balaam's advice and were the means of turning the Israelites away from the LORD in what happened at Peor, so that a plague struck the LORD's people" (Numbers 31:16, NIV).

Balaam knew that if the people began to sin sexually it would cause a rift in their relationship with God, and that is exactly what happened! In Numbers 25:1–3 (NLT), we read: "While the Israelites were camped at Acacia Grove, some of the men defiled themselves by having sexual relations with local Moabite women. These women invited them to attend sacrifices to their gods, so the Israelites feasted with them and worshiped the gods of Moab. In this way, Israel joined in the worship of Baal of Peor, causing the LORD's anger

"SEXUAL SIN SEPARATES YOU FROM A HOLY GOD."

to blaze against his people." Balaam did exactly what Jezebel did. She introduced people to the compromise of idolatry and sexual sin. This is very important for you to understand. *Sexual sin separates you from a holy God.*

Nothing can separate us from God's love, but this doesn't mean we can walk with God and live in sin at the same time. In Romans 1:24-25 (NLT), we read: "So God abandoned them to do whatever shameful things their hearts desired. As a result, they did vile and degrading things with each other's bodies. They traded the truth about God for a lie. So they worshiped and served the things God created instead of the Creator himself, who is worthy of eternal praise! Amen." People are choosing sexual sin over their relationship with God. God is jealous for you (Exodus 34:14). You cannot be sexually intimate with the world (Jezebel) and intimate with God at the same time!

"YOU CANNOT BE SEXUALLY INTIMATE WITH THE WORLD (JEZEBEL) AND INTIMATE WITH GOD AT THE SAME TIME!"

Homosexuality was a practice in Jezebel's religion, and male prostitutes served in the temples of Baal. Jezebel is an advocate for homosexuality. She supports the homosexual agenda. It is a part of her religion. Why? Simply because God made man and woman and told them to reproduce. In Genesis 1:27-28 (NIV), we read: "So God created man in his own image, in the image of God he created him; male and female he created them. God blessed them and said to them, 'Be fruitful and increase in number; fill the earth and subdue it.'" Satan immediately went to work to destroy what God had created. Satan can only destroy, not create.

Like Jezebel, Satanism promotes sexual worship. A common statement attributed to the Church of Satan's founder, Anton LaVey, is: "Satanism is pro-sexuality. Sexuality is a pure form of pleasure, something that satisfies our deepest purpose in life. Modern life allows us to enjoy sex without the risks of unplanned pregnancies and sexual diseases assuming that sense is taken. Which it should be. Satanism supports any fetish, kink or flavor of sexual encounter as long as all parties involved are consenting." Satan reverses God's order to mock God. First Peter 1:16 (NIV) says, "for it is written: 'Be holy, because I am holy.'" God tells us to be holy, so Satan encourages us to pursue sexual promiscuity! Satanists are known to recite the Lord's Prayer backwards to begin their services, a reverse of God's Word to defy His divine order. Reverse sexual orientation is the reverse of God's established order and it mocks God.

Rainbows are a sign of God's covenant on the clouds of judgment, but they are now waved with pride by those who practice homosexuality. In Genesis 9:13 (NIV), we read, "I have set my rainbow in the clouds, and it will be the sign of the covenant between me and the earth." *Pride* has become the homosexual slogan, and is also the main source that drives the spirit of Jezebel! In James 4:6-7 (NLT), we read: "'God opposes the proud but gives grace to the humble.' Submit yourselves, then, to God. Resist the devil, and he will flee from you." Pride is the enemy of God. Jezebel is the enemy of God. Homosexuals cannot produce, they cannot reproduce, and they cannot bear fruit! In Matthew 12:33, we read, "Make a tree good and its fruit will be good, or make a tree bad and its fruit will be bad, for a tree is recognized by its fruit." Jezebel has no spiritual fruit!

Much of the time, ministers and Christian leaders do a poor job with this topic. People have made it about, "Does God love you (them) or not?" So let's be clear: God loves you. He loves the homosexual sinner. He loves the heterosexual sinner. He loves sinners! In Romans 5:8 (NIV), we read, "But God demonstrates his own love for us in this: While we were still sinners, Christ died for us." He loves us, no matter what! *God loves everyone, but He changes His standards of morality for no one!* We're not talking about whether God loves us or anyone else, He does. What we are talking about is, do you (or they) love Him? Because if you love Him, you will obey Him. John 14:15 (NIV) says, "If you love me, you will obey what I command."

"GOD LOVES EVERYONE, BUT HE CHANGES HIS STANDARDS OF MORALITY FOR NO ONE!"

Murdering those who disagreed with her, Jezebel silenced the voices of the prophets. In 1 Kings 18:4 (NLT), we read: "Once when Jezebel had tried to kill all the LORD's prophets, Obadiah had hidden 100 of them in two caves." The homosexual agenda behaves like Jezebel. It wages war on those who voice a different opinion than theirs, especially a biblical opinion. Our nation is now in legal battles, calling it hate speech if you morally object to homosexuality. Jezebel is removing any voice that would oppose her agenda, through intimidation.

The homosexual population statistics have been exaggerated for decades. They want it to appear that there are more of them than there really are. The mass minority has influenced the majority because the majority think they are all alone. Elijah thought the very same way. In 1 Kings 19:14 (NLT), we read: "He replied again, 'I have zealously served the LORD God Almighty. But the people of Israel have broken their covenant with you, torn down your altars, and killed every one of your prophets. I am the only one left, and now they are trying to kill me, too.'"

Tolerance has become a slogan of the world that the church has begun to adopt as their own. Some ministers are *fearful* of losing their tax exempt status if they preach biblically on God's stance on marriage (Matthew 19:5), or perform marriage ceremonies because of new marriage equality laws. Maybe Jesus was warning this of day when he told us to "give to Caesar what belongs to Caesar" (Mark 12:17, NLT).

It is no coincidence that over 2000 years ago, God would know our future conversations. He knew people today would debate and argue, claiming: "Homosexuals can't help it. They were born the way they are!" That's why He said, "you must be born again!" In John 3:7 (NIV), we read, "You should not be surprised at my saying, 'You must be born again.'" It doesn't matter how you were born, according to Jesus, you must be born again!

The first mention of Baal is found in the Book of Exodus. This was a significant moment in the lives of Moses, Aaron, and the Children of Israel. In Exodus 32:19 (NIV), we read, "When Moses approached the camp and saw the calf and the dancing, his anger burned and he threw the tablets out of his hands, breaking them to pieces at the foot of the mountain." The spirit of Jezebel had intimidated and influenced Aaron to make a statue and the Children of Israel began to worship, dance naked, and engage in sexual acts. Exodus 32:25 (NIV) says, "Moses saw that the people were running wild and that Aaron had let them get out of control and so become a laughingstock to their enemies." We don't want Christians to become the laughing-stock of the world. We must practice what we preach.

I was in India recently, holding a crusade. I was asked by the leading apostle over the host ministry not to teach on the topic of marriage. I wasn't planning on speaking on marriage. I was planning on teaching on the power of the Holy Spirit, but out of curiosity I asked him why. He said, "The people of India know that Americans have the highest divorce rate in the world. How can you teach them what you do not do?" This is a problem. How can Christians teach the world about holiness when we don't live it? Through compromise we have strayed far from the holy God we claim to serve.

When clothes are coming off and the wedding bed is being defiled, the spirit of Jezebel is involved. Exodus 32:25 says the people were "running wild." In the Hebrew, that phrase, e*rwâ* indicates *various stages of undress, from being inappropriately clad to being totally nude.* They were worshiping Baal, naked! They were exposing their private, vulnerable parts to Baal. The word, *nakedness*, is very important to look at. Why does Jezebel want you naked?

In the beginning, Adam and Eve were naked in the Garden of Eden: "Now the man and his wife were both naked, but they felt no shame" (Genesis 2:25, NLT). They had no shame because they were in right standing with God. They were in a state of innocence. As we learned in Chapter 6, the spirit of Jezebel (through the serpent) deceived Eve into sin. Instantaneously, Adam and Eve became aware of their nakedness and attempted to cover themselves: "Then the eyes of both of them were opened, and they knew that they were naked; and they sewed fig leaves together and made themselves coverings" (Genesis 3:7, NKJV). They tried to cover their nakedness. They tried to cover their shame. But they didn't have the ability to cover their own guilt, so they ran away and hid from God. In Genesis 3:9-10 (NKJV), we read: "Then the LORD God called to Adam and said to him, 'Where are you?' So he said, 'I heard Your voice in the garden, and I was afraid because I was naked; and I hid myself.'"

Nakedness is correlated with shame throughout the Scriptures. The naked body was taboo in Hebrew society, perhaps in part because bodily fluids were considered unclean (Leviticus 15:12). In Hebrew usage *nakedness* is often a euphemism for sexual relations (Ezekiel 16:18). Nakedness was forbidden in Israelite religious ceremonies, largely because of its association with Canaanite rites. In Leviticus 20:23 (NLT), we read: "You must not live according to the customs of the nations I am going to drive out before you. Because they did all these things, I abhorred them." Public nakedness was normally considered an occasion for shame—a characteristic of the prostitute or the adulteress. In Revelation 17:16, we read: "The beast and the ten horns you saw will hate the prostitute. They will bring her to ruin and leave her naked; they will eat her flesh and burn her with fire." The Gospel accounts of the crucifixion record that the soldiers who crucified Christ divided his garments, leaving him naked: "When the soldiers crucified Jesus, they took his clothes, dividing them into four shares, one for each of them, with the undergarment remaining. This garment was seamless, woven in one piece from top to bottom" (John 19:23, NIV). Jesus was crucified, naked, in shame, and exposed for us. He took away the shame of the world on the cross.

Taking the Fall

Tim was twenty years old and he served as the youth pastor at his dad's church. One weekend, their church hosted a very large community service. Tim's dad approached the stage to welcome the congregation. As he walked up to the pulpit, he slipped on the top step and fell very hard on the stage. The entire church gasped, watching closely to see if he was going to be okay. He brushed it off with class and went on with the service, but Tim could tell that he was really embarrassed. (This would be embarrassing for anyone.)

It was Tim's responsibility to take up the offering that day. As Tim walked up the stairs, he purposefully placed the edge of his dress shoe on the corner of the wooden steps, knowing it would cause him to fall. A second later, he was flat on his back in front of hundreds of people. Once again, the church responded with concern. Tim got up very slowly, having landed much harder than he had anticipated, saying into the microphone, "Someone really needs to fix these steps." Tim didn't want the last image the church remembered to be one of their pastor fallen and embarrassed.

When Jesus died on the cross, He became the last image of nakedness and shame. In Genesis 3:21 (NLT), we read, "And the LORD God made clothing from animal skins for Adam and his wife." Just as in the Garden of Eden, on the cross Jesus wanted to take upon Himself your nakedness and shame so that when people looked at you, they would not remember your nakedness, but His.

Jezebel is all about exposing you! Exposing your private, intimate, vulnerable parts to Baal and self-worship is her goal. Taking our clothes off in an act of defilement and sin is extremely significant because it takes us all the way back to the Garden of Eden. When we remove our clothes in unauthorized sexual acts, we remove the covering of Christ that He gave us on the cross.

Adam and Eve's sin, like ours, is what separates us from God. God was looking for them but they pulled away from Him because of their transgressions. This is how the spirit of Jezebel will pull you away from God. You can never cover your sin by yourself, no matter how hard you try! No matter how hard you try to ignore it, or distract yourself from it, you can't cover it up—only Jesus can!

Back to Moses. In Exodus 32:26 (NIV), we read: "So he stood at the entrance to the camp and said, 'Whoever is for the LORD, come to me.' And all the Levites rallied to him." It is interesting, how he uses this phrase against the spirit of Jezebel. Elijah used a similar phrase when he battled Jezebel. In 1 Kings 18:20-21 (NLT), we read, "So Ahab summoned all the people of Israel and the prophets to Mount Carmel. Then Elijah stood in front of them and said, 'How much longer will you waver, hobbling between two opinions? If the LORD is God, follow him! But if Baal is God, then follow him!' But the people were completely silent."

The Body of Christ has not only been tolerant of sexual perversion—it has embraced it. And we are suffering for it! Revelation 2:20-22 (NIV) reads: "Nevertheless, I have this against you: You tolerate that woman Jezebel, who calls herself a prophetess. By her teaching she misleads my servants into sexual immorality and the eating of food sacrificed to idols. I have given her time to repent of her immorality, but she is unwilling. So I will cast her on a bed of suffering, and I will make those who commit adultery with her suffer intensely, unless they repent of her ways." We can no longer tolerate tolerance to sexual immorality. When the heart of true repentance comes to God's house and His people, it will bring us back to intimacy with God. Who is on the Lord's side?

If you have fallen prey to the seduction of the spirit of Jezebel it's a good time to stop and pray.

Lord Jesus, I ask you to forgive me of all of my sin. I ask you to cleanse me of all unrighteousness. Forgive me for sinning sexually against myself and your holiness. I ask for you to help me resist these sins of my flesh. Lord, be made strong in this weakness of mine. I rebuke this spirit of Jezebel. I denounce all sexual sin. Holy Spirit, help me flee from all temptation. The Lord rebuke you Satan, and every lie from the pit of hell. Father, show me my true identity as a son/daughter. I ask you for a new heart a new mind and clean spirit. Father, help me to live a life of holiness and purity before you. Amen.

Dealing With Jezebel: Do's and Don'ts

Do: Live a life with a high standard of righteousness and integrity. Tell others of these standards to keep you accountable to them.

Don't: Don't hide your own sexual temptations and sin. Confess them. This will protect you from being seduced into sexual sin by Jezebel.

CHAPTER 10

JEZEBEL HAS FRIENDS
(FAMILIAR SPIRITS)

There are other spirits that often work in collaboration with the spirit of Jezebel. These are powerful, manipulative spirits that set themselves up as strongholds that often go undetected in the lives of Christians. These are spirits that focus on fear, past mistakes and failures, shame, money, selfishness, anxiety, idolatry, and more. When Jezebel is around, these spirits are not too far away.

The Spirit of Faultfinder

The spirit of faultfinder is a powerful, accusatory spirit that spreads lies and casts doubt in the hearts of spectators. When Jezebel is confronted or close to being exposed, the spirit of faultfinder goes to work, making it appear as if there are faults in you or others. If anyone resists her, she will find fault in them. If anyone confronts her, she will find fault in them. If anyone opposes her, she will place a fault on them. Jezebel places faults on people that are simply not there!

"Are you the king of Israel or not?" Jezebel demanded. "Get up and eat something, and don't worry about it. I'll get you Naboth's vineyard!" So she wrote letters in Ahab's name, sealed them with his seal, and sent them to the elders and other leaders of the town where Naboth lived. In her letters she commanded: "Call the citizens together for fasting and prayer, and give Naboth a place of honor. And then seat two scoundrels across from him who will accuse him of cursing God and the king. Then take him out and stone him to death." (1 Kings 21:7-10, NLT)

Wow, this is so evil! Jezebel intentionally sets Naboth up. She places a fault on him that wasn't really there. Many times, a person operating in the Jezebel spirit wants something another person has. It could be a spot on the frontline worship team, a teaching ministry position, a relationship, a position at work, or any number of other things. She will find the fault so she can come in and take what she wants.

Jezebel is a master projectionist. She will project onto others what's really in her. She will say things about others like, "I think she just has a bad heart." Really? A bad heart? She says this about a person who volunteers in the church twenty hours a week, takes time off work to serve there, gets no pay or recognition. This person has a bad heart? This faithful, humble servant may have a bad heart, but Jezebel does. She has wrong motives too, so she place faults on others so no one ever looks at her.

Faultfinders usually start faultfinding with questions or statements like this: "What do you think about *that person*?" or, "I don't know...there is just something about her..." These questions of suspicion are asked with the intent to place fault.

In Genesis 3:1 (NLT), we read: "The serpent was the shrewdest of all the wild animals the LORD God had made. One day he asked the woman, 'Did God really say you must not eat the fruit from any of the trees in the garden?'" God had just given Adam and Eve specific instructions on how to obey Him and immediately, Satan asked them a question, preparing a fault that he had set up through temptation. In another example, Satan asked God a question about Job to try to find fault in him. In Job 1:9-11 (NIV), we read: "'Does Job fear God for nothing?' Satan replied. 'Have you not put a hedge around him and his household and everything he has? You have blessed the work of his hands, so that his flocks and herds are spread throughout the land. But stretch out your hand and strike everything he has, and he will surely curse you to your face.'" This was diabolical. Satan was accusing him of a fault that *he* had created!

The spirit of faultfinder is the same spirit we call "the accuser of the brethren." In Revelation 12:10 (NLT), we read: "Then I heard a loud voice shouting across the heavens, 'It has come at last salvation and power and the Kingdom of our God, and the authority of his Christ. For the accuser of our brothers and sisters has been thrown down to earth the one who accuses them before our God day and night.'"

Faultfinders like to bring up your past. Watch how this works. When you are completely submitted to Jezebel's control, everything in your past is your "testimony." It's all under the blood and everything is behind you. But if you cross her, your past becomes fair game. Everything you did, said, or experienced will be used against you!

The Fault That Wasn't There

At one time, Matthew walked through a very challenging season in his life. He was an executive missions coordinator at a growing missions organization and he regularly covered the group teaching for his lead director. Matthew was in the fight of his life, battling the spirit of Jezebel for the first time after becoming fully aware of it. Matthew's relationship with his director had become hostile. It seemed as if he was always upset with Matthew, though when Matthew pressed him about it to see if he had offended him or done wrong, his director couldn't come up with anything that hadn't already been dealt with way in the past; nothing for which he had not forgiven Matthew. The relationship deteriorated to the point where he was unreceptive in all their interactions. Matthew realized they needed outside assistance to help resolve their situation and find peace.

Matthew reached out to the head residing board member to help facilitate a phone meeting. Once on the phone, Matthew's director spoke first, going over his list of complaints, fast and furious. None of his complaints had any substance. He had no proof to support his accusations. The board member pressed the director for firm proof of his complaints against Matthew. Finally, the director blurted out, "Matthew has a homosexual living with him!" Matthew couldn't believe his ears! Matthew was so upset and deeply hurt by this accusation, he was shaking. Matthew's wife was with him on the phone call and her jaw dropped when the director said it.

The board member asked Matthew to respond to the comment. Matthew began to explain: "My wife and I have a heart for hurting people. A good friend called me last year and asked me to help his brother because he was falling into a pretty heavy sinful lifestyle. My wife and I prayed about it and both were in agreement that he needed to come live with us as we disciple him through his deliverance process." Then Matthew stopped and said to the director, "Sir, you know all of this!" The director was aware of every detail of the story, but the faultfinder launched accusations.

Those who know Jesus and live Christ-centered lives keep no record of wrong (1 Corinthians 13:5). Jezebel keeps records of wrong and accuses us of wrong we haven't even committed yet. Godly men and women find the best in people. The spirit of faultfinder will always find the worst.

"GODLY MEN AND WOMEN FIND THE BEST IN PEOPLE. THE SPIRIT OF FAULTFINDER WILL ALWAYS FIND THE WORST."

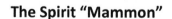

The Spirit "Mammon"

You have heard the saying, "money is power." Jezebel loves power, so if money helps gain more power, she loves it as well. Jezebel is drawn to the rich, using them for their money. It's amazing to see how many Christian leaders ignore Scripture when it comes to money and rich, affluent people. In James 2:3-4 (NLT), we read: "If you give special attention and a good seat to the rich person, but you say to the poor one, 'You can stand over there, or else sit on the floor'—well, doesn't this discrimination show that your judgments are guided by evil motives?" In some cases, rich people have better seats, reserved parking spots, a fast track to meetings with the leadership, and more. They are treated as if they are more important than others. Why? Because of what they bring to the table.

Jezebel doesn't have right motives and she doesn't have a pure heart, so she's drawn to what appears to make her look better in the eyes of other people. Jezebel also uses money to control people. Money is an inanimate object, and is neither good nor bad because it's not alive. It depends on whose hands it's in. A gun in the hand of a police officer is typically a good thing. That same gun in the hand of a criminal is a destructive thing. The intentions of the person holding it determines if it is good or evil. In 1 Timothy 6:10, we read: "For the love of money is a root of all kinds of evil. Some people, eager for money, have wandered from the faith and pierced themselves with many griefs." Money is not evil. The love of money is evil. The Bible teaches us to never allow the spirit of money to control us. In Hebrews 13:5, we read, "Keep your lives free from the love of money and be content with what you have."

Jezebel loves to keep people dependent upon her. You see this in ministries that teach a polluted prosperity message, where the only person prospering in the church is the one manipulating the message. Now let me be extremely clear. I believe in prosperity. I believe it's biblical (3 John 1:2). I believe money can be used to advance the Gospel and help people, just as we see in the examples in the Book of Acts. I just don't believe in manipulation of any kind. But Jezebel does believe in it and manipulates through money. We call this "mammon"!

Mammon is the evil spirit behind money. The Bible only mentions the word, *mammon*, in two places, Matthew 6:24 and Luke 16:9-13.

In Matthew 6:24 (NKJV), we read: "No man can serve two masters: for either he will hate the one, and love the other; or else he will hold to the one, and despise the other. Ye cannot serve God and mammon." Mammon is a transliteration of the Aramaic word, *māmÙn*, which simply means *wealth, profit,* or *riches.* Mammon was the Assyrian god of riches. They adopted their god from the Babylonians. The Babylonians were most known for their construction of the Tower of Babel. *Babel* is where we get the word *Baal.*

In Genesis 11:3-4 (NLT), we read: "They began saying to each other, 'Let's make bricks and harden them with fire.' Then they said, 'Come, let's build a great city for ourselves with a tower that reaches into the sky. This will make us famous and keep us from being scattered all over the world.'" They were making a tower to get to heaven by themselves, without God—in fact, in spite of Him! Mammon attempts to take the place of God. Sound familiar? It should because it's a familiar spirit that works in perfect harmony with Jezebel. If you have great wealth (mammon) it is easy to kid yourself and ask, "Why do I need God?" You think you have circumvented Him. You begin to trust in your money instead of your God (Proverbs 3:5).

Mammon wants a platform in your life. Mammon becomes the filter by which you determine what you will and will not do for God. You begin to tell God how much it will cost Him for you to work for Him. You tell Him how you can't do a certain ministry, project, or business because you don't have enough money. Then you start putting a price tag on God!

I'm in Sin

One day, sitting in my living room, I studied this topic, mammon. I had researched everything I just shared with you and was focusing particularly on how the spirit of mammon works. Just like Jezebel, mammon operates in fear: fear of not having enough and fear of running out of what you do have. I realized that I was always worried, nervous about how I was going to cover all my needs financially. In that moment of realization, I heard the Lord speak to me, saying "You serve mammon!" I was floored when I heard this and a bit confused. The Lord said, "Mammon is any amount of money you compare to me." In that very moment, I got it.

I had always given God a dollar amount I needed for me to work for a cause in His name. From TV shows to networks to missions projects, I had always told God the amount I needed to serve Him. I didn't allow God to creatively work miracles in my life because I had given Him my price tags. This was mammon. I had trained myself to think I needed either "x" number of dollars or God needed to do a miracle. I needed mammon (money) or God. I had placed mammon on the same altar with God.

Then God began to remind me how, throughout His Word, He provided for His children through creative miracles. He provided through a creative miracle in Luke 5:4-7, when the disciples cast their nets on the other side of their boats as Jesus instructed them. They caught so many fish their nets began to break! He provided through a creative miracle in 2 Kings 4:3-7, when a widow woman poured oil which miraculously multiplied to fill every jar she had, enabling her to purchase her sons out of slavery. He provided through a creative miracle in Exodus 17:6-7, when water came from a rock to quench the thirst of the Children of Israel. He provided through a creative miracle in Luke 19:31, when a colt was provided as transportation for His ministry. God does creative miracles!

I fell on my face on the carpet of my living room and repented for allowing the spirit of mammon to have authority over my life. From that day on, I was very aware of the authority of mammon and the influence it had on my life. Every day, I rebuked it and submitted to the creative power of God. A few months after that experience, someone donated all the technology to launch my online TV network. God creatively provided!

You don't need money. You need only creative miracles. Miracles make mammon and Jezebel bow down. Jezebel wanted Baal, like mammon, to have a place on God's altar. In 1 Kings 18:23-24 (NLT), we read: "Now bring two bulls. The prophets of Baal may choose whichever one they wish and cut it into pieces and lay it on the wood of their altar, but without setting fire to it. I will prepare the other bull and lay it on the wood on the altar, but not set fire to it. Then call on the name of your god, and I will call on the name of the LORD. The god who answers by setting fire to the wood is the true God!' And all the people agreed." Baal simply being on the altar, like mammon, was an option for worship. Whoever provided first, they would worship. Jezebel wants to distract us from worshiping the true God. She works with mammon (money) to so distract us that it gains our full attention, rather than God.

"MIRACLES MAKE MAMMON AND JEZEBEL BOW DOWN."

Money-driven people are selfish people. Jezebel is a self-pleasing, self-worshiper. Jezebel and mammon have one last major similarity: They never put people first. Let's look at the second scripture that mentions the spirit of mammon. In Luke 16:9-11 (NKJV), we read: "And I say to you, make friends for yourselves by unrighteous mammon, that when you fail, they may receive you into an everlasting home. He who is faithful in what is least is faithful also in much; and he who is unjust in what is least is unjust also in much. Therefore if you have not been faithful in the unrighteous mammon, who will commit to your trust the true riches?" I've heard it taught for years: If you're faithful with a little bit of money, God will make you a ruler over much money. I believe God is saying something much deeper here. I believe that a little money and a lot of money is still just money.

I believe this scripture shows us that if we can overcome the spirit of mammon that is *"all money,"* He will give us "true riches," that is, people. Mammon puts money above people. Jezebel puts herself above other people, but I believe God would have of us break these spirits by *putting people first.*

It is easy to break free from the spirit of mammon. Simply repent and strive to be intentionally generous (Psalm 37:26). Look for opportunities to donate, and when you do, give joyfully (2 Corinthians 9:7). Ask yourself on a regular basis, "Am I generous?" Ask people you trust the same question. Unfortunately, the spirit of mammon is harder to stay free from than to break free from. Rebuke the spirit of mammon out loud every time you start to feel greedy or worry about money. Ask God to teach you how to trust Him and bless you in order for you to bless others. Pray about ministries and causes to support. Give things away. Exercise a spirit of generosity!

Dealing With Jezebel: Do's and Don'ts

Do: Do not believe everything people say about others, make sure you are not allowing faultfinder to deceive you.

Don't: Don't accept any favors or gifts from Jezebel. Don't accept anything that would cause you to owe her any favors or be indebted to her.

CHAPTER 11

KILL THE MESSENGER

Let's begin to corner Jezebel strategically and challenge some major methods she uses to inflict fear on her victims. Jezebel uses people to transport messages of fear through words. Messengers are dispatched with her words of witchcraft. People are sometimes even unaware that Jezebel is using them. When you stop the messenger, you stop her message.

We have covered the power of words in this book. We have explored the power of words and their effects. Now let's look more closely at the vehicle of transportation for her words. Jezebel doesn't care about people, so of course she has no issue with using people to transport her words of witchcraft. The Bible refers to these messengers as *eunuchs* or servants. The Hebrew word for *messenger* is *malak*, which means: *a messenger who runs on foot, the bearer of dispatches. One who bears a message or does an errand; an employee who carries messages.* In the Christian church world, we might be more familiar with the word, *message*, as it is often used in place of the word, *sermon*. We often say, "Pastor, that was a great message." In Malachi 2:7, we read, "For the lips of a priest ought to preserve knowledge, and from his mouth men should seek instruction—because he is the messenger of the LORD Almighty." Whereas a pastor prepares a message of hope laced with love to release the Spirit of God into the hearts of God's people, Jezebel prepares a message of despair to release fear into those very same hearts.

The word, *angel*, is derived from the Greek word, *angelos*, which means *a messenger*. We find accounts of angelic beings bringing messages to God's people throughout the Bible. In Hebrews 2:2

> ## "Whereas a pastor prepares a message of hope laced with love to release the Spirit of God into the hearts of God's people, Jezebel prepares a message of despair to release fear into those very same hearts."

(NLT), we read, "For the message God delivered through angels has always stood firm, and every violation of the law and every act of disobedience was punished." The word, *apostle*, comes from a Greek word meaning, *sent*. These are men sent to deliver words from God to a specific audience. In Jeremiah 1:7-8 (NLT), we read: "The LORD replied, 'Don't say, "I'm too young," for you must go wherever I send you and say whatever I tell you. And don't be afraid of the people, for I will be with you and will protect you. I, the LORD, have spoken!'" Just as God uses people as instruments to deliver messages from Him, Jezebel uses people to deliver messages from her.

Many people unwarily deliver Jezebel's message for her. She subtly spreads her message to her messengers. What would you say if you were standing on a street corner and someone came up and asked you to deliver a package to a certain address for $100? You would probably say, "No way!" or "What's in it?" We deliver Jezebel's message through gossip, slander, and *by repeating her words*. When someone operating in the spirit of Jezebel tells you information about others, you need to stop them and say, "I don't care to hear one more word." You need to be extremely careful with the messages you tell people because you don't always know what's in them.

Security

I'm sitting in coach, near the back of an airplane as I write this chapter. I'm flying internationally, back to New York. No less than five times in the ridiculously long security process, I am asked, "Have you had possession of your bag at all times?" Each and every time I replied, "Yes!" At one point, my traveling companion and I look at one another and laugh as we were asked the same question three times while walking twenty feet of the security line.

Airline officials wanted to make sure we knew what we were carrying. It was a matter of national security. It's a matter of spiritual security that you know the origin and originator of the words you share with people. Do not be careless with your words or the words of others. In Matthew 12:36 (NIV), we read, "But I tell you that men will have to give account on the day of judgment for every careless word they have spoken."

A good rule of thumb is, if someone starts telling you something by saying, "Well, I'm not sure if I should be saying this," stop them right there. Don't participate in transporting their message. If someone tells you, "I'm going to tell you something, but you have to *promise* me, you won't tell anyone," it is manipulation. To agree causes you to be bound by your promise to hold the message. When someone says this to you, interrupt them, saying, "I'm sorry, I can't do that." Then if they keep talking, you are not a prisoner of manipulation.

Look at what the Bible says God hates: "There are six things the LORD hates, seven that are detestable to him: haughty eyes, a lying tongue, hands that shed innocent blood, a heart that devises wicked schemes, feet that are quick to rush into evil, a false witness who pours out lies and a man who stirs up dissension among brothers" (Proverbs 6:16-19, NIV). Three of the seven things the Lord detests come from men's mouths! Why is this so important? Because Jezebel's messengers are not transporting words alone, they are transporting her spirit! Her message is for anyone who will listen to it—anyone naïve enough to pick up the package and carry it to its destination.

She looks for those who are rebellious, who resist and resent author-ity, who complain, are bitter, offended, disgruntled, or are gossips. Like a suicide bomber carrying an explosive device designed to hurt people, Jezebel's messengers transport her words to cause mass casualty damage.

"...JEZEBEL'S MESSENGERS ARE NOT TRANSPORTING WORDS ALONE, THEY ARE TRANSPORTING HER SPIRIT!"

I've always found it interesting how people who leave a church or ministry on bad terms are automatically drawn to others who also left. Suddenly, they become the best of friends. The majority of the time, they were friends when they attended the former church. Sometimes they didn't even like each other. Their friendships are based on a mutual adversary, not on mutual friendship and love for one another. I have always advised people, "If you weren't close with people before you left the ministry, be careful how soon you let them in after you leave." Just because someone left a church you left does not mean you should be getting advice from them. They tend to have Jezebel's message instead of godly counsel.

This is not unlike politics. Not many people seem to be for a par-ticular candidate as much as they seem to be against another who is running. Typically, they hate the president or the governor, so they support the candidate who is running against him or her. This is why approval ratings are always so low. When the person who ran against the candidate they didn't like gets elected, they were not really for him or her in the first place, so their support is short-lived. This is also why relationships birthed from a common enemy or adversary don't last long. Listening to Jezebel's message empowers it. Speaking Jezebel's message spreads it. *Listeners become messengers!*

"LISTENERS BECOME MESSENGERS!"

When equipped with Jezebel's message, these servants spread the very same witchcraft as Jezebel herself.

> Now Ahab told Jezebel everything Elijah had done and how he had killed all the prophets with the sword. So Jezebel sent a messenger to Elijah to say, "May the gods deal with me, be it ever so severely, if by this time tomorrow I do not make your life like that of one of them." Elijah was afraid and ran for his life. When he came to Beersheba in Judah, he left his servant there, while he himself went a day's journey into the desert. He came to a broom tree, sat down under it and prayed that he might die. "I have had enough, LORD," he said. "Take my life; I am no better than my ancestors." (1 Kings 19:1-4)

Jezebel never spoke directly to Elijah. They never met in person. She spoke to Elijah through a messenger. The message, produced in fear, landed in the heart of God's prophet, sending him spiraling off course. Her demonic message turned Elijah's victory into fear, doubt, confusion, intimidation, and discouragement. He felt the impact of her witchcraft. The Apostle Paul felt the same impact of a demonic messenger. In 2 Corinthians 12:7, we read, "To keep me from becoming conceited because of these surpassingly great revelations, there was given me a thorn in my flesh, a messenger of Satan, to torment me." Even when delivered through her messengers, Jezebel's messages will inflict torment. When her message was considered by Elijah, confusion took over. He pondered Jezebel's message, wondering if it could really be true. Fear took over!

The historical phrase, "Don't kill the messenger," describes a breach in the understood code of conduct between commanding officers in wartime. These officers were expected to receive and return unharmed any emissaries or diplomatic envoys sent by the enemy. Established during the early Warring States period of China (between 475 and 221 BCE), this concept of chivalry and virtue prevented the execution of messengers sent by opposing sides. Soldiers were forbidden to kill messengers of war.

Shakespeare brought the term from the battlefield to a mainstream audience in his play, *Henry IV, Part 2* (1598). In this drama, when Cleopatra gets the bad news that Antony has married Octavia, she becomes angry, actually striking and threatening the messenger, who explains, "Gracious madam, I that do bring the news made not the match."[3] This phrase has become popular over the years and many have used it to divert the wrath of their audience.

When it comes to Jezebel, I want to admonish you to kill the messenger! Jezebel's messengers extend the reach of her witchcraft. Her messengers expand her kingdom. Her messengers are in training to become Jezebels of their own. You kill the messenger by not allowing him/her to finish sentences. You kill the messenger by not reading poisonous emails. You kill the messenger by rebuking gossip,

"YOU KILL THE MESSENGER BY NOT ALLOWING HIM/HER TO FINISH SENTENCES."

stopping it right in its tracks. You kill the messenger by refusing to repeat any of her words to anyone!

Elijah learned from his mistakes the first time around and quickly altered his strategy. He would never again allow a messenger from Jezebel to bring him words of fear! Watch how he let God deal with Jezebel's messengers.

> After Ahab's death, Moab rebelled against Israel. Now Ahaziah had fallen through the lattice of his upper room in Samaria and injured himself. So he sent messengers, saying to them, "Go and consult Baal-Zebub, the god of Ekron, to see if I will recover from this injury." But the angel of the LORD said to Elijah the Tishbite, "Go up and meet the messengers of the king of Samaria and ask them, 'Is it because there is no God in Israel that you are going off to consult Baal-Zebub, the god of Ekron?' Therefore this is what the LORD says: 'You will not leave the bed you are lying on. You will certainly die!'" So Elijah went. When the messengers returned to the king, he asked them, "Why have you come back?" "A man came to meet us," they replied. "And he said to us, 'Go back to the king who sent you and tell him, "This is what the LORD says: Is it because there is no God in Israel that you are sending men to consult Baal-Zebub, the god of Ekron? Therefore you will not leave the bed you are lying on. You will certainly die!"'" The king asked them, "What kind of man was it who came to meet you and told you this?" They replied, "He was a man with a garment of hair and with a leather belt around his waist." The king said, "That was Elijah the Tishbite." Then he sent to Elijah a captain with his company of fifty men. The captain went up to Elijah, who was sitting on the top of a hill, and said to him, "Man of God, the king says, 'Come down!' " Elijah answered the captain, "If I am a man of God, may fire come down from heaven and consume you and your fifty men!" Then fire fell from heaven and consumed the captain and his men. At this

the king sent to Elijah another captain with his fifty men. The captain said to him, "Man of God, this is what the king says, 'Come down at once!' " "If I am a man of God," Elijah replied, "may fire come down from heaven and consume you and your fifty men!" Then the fire of God fell from heaven and consumed him and his fifty men. So the king sent a third captain with his fifty men. This third captain went up and fell on his knees before Elijah. "Man of God," he begged, "please have respect for my life and the lives of these fifty men, your servants! See, fire has fallen from heaven and consumed the first two captains and all their men. But now have respect for my life!" (2 Kings 1:1-14)

The fear of God came upon this final messenger. He said to himself, *Even though the king (spirit of Jezebel) sent me, I will not deliver the message!* It takes an amazing amount of grace and spiritual discernment to realize when you have become a conduit of the messages of Jezebel.

Refusing to repeat Jezebel's words is the first step in stopping and eventually defeating her. When you cut off her messengers you stop her from spreading her witchcraft. Stopping her messengers can be difficult but is very doable when you are aware of what's going on spiritually.

Stopping Jezebel's message in you isn't so easy. (Yes, in you!) You spread the words of witchcraft when you tell others what Jezebel did or said about you or and over you! Not repeating her words can be so difficult. It brings a false sense of comfort to call a close friend to just "confide" in him or her. Some of us who are very "spiritually mature" call this "venting." We desire to be justified. We want to be vindicated, but we can never be vindicated by man, only God. This might sound a bit firm, but you need to hear it. If you have the need to tell others what Jezebel (or others) said about you, it is because there is spiritual weakness in your life. Jezebel lies because she hates (Proverbs 10:18). Don't spread her lies by repeating them to anyone!

I'm not saying there are some matters that don't need to be dealt with. I'm not saying all matters are the same. I am saying there is a proper way to handle them. First, whenever you are dealing with Jezebel's words, you should respond vertically, not horizontally. To respond horizontally is to spread her message of lies to people on your same level: peers, friends, co-workers, and so on. To respond vertically is to take them upward to your spiritually authority (mentors, pastors), but most importantly, to God Himself. Learn how to allow God to comfort your spirit and how not to depend so much on the comfort and encouragement of other people.

King David learned how to do this very thing. In 1 Samuel 30:6 (NLT), we read: "David was now in great danger because all his men were very bitter about losing their sons and daughters, and they began to talk of stoning him. But David found strength in the LORD his God." You know you are growing and maturing spiritually when you get your strength from God.

Elijah learned from his mistakes. He had gained spiritual ground against Jezebel. He anointed Elisha to succeed him as prophet, and anointed Jehu as king and executioner of Jezebel. Jehu would stop at nothing to see Jezebel defeated. Elijah confronted Jezebel's messengers, but Jehu wouldn't allow them to even finish their sentences. When you've silenced Jezebel's messengers, it leaves one last thing to deal with, Jezebel herself.

Dealing With Jezebel: Do's and Don'ts

Do: Rebuke every lie spoken to you and over you, every time you hear one.

Don't: Don't give in to the need to tell other people what Jezebel has said about you or over you.

CHAPTER 12

DEALING WITH AND
DEFEATING JEZEBEL

It's time to deal with and defeat Jezebel. When the spirit of Jezebel is exposed, it leaves only two options: surrender to her or resist her. But for those who serve the Lord, there is really only one option. Jesus admonishes us not to tolerate Jezebel any longer (Revelations 2:20). It takes a warrior spirit to confront and deal with Jezebel. Jehu was a man driven to no longer tolerate Jezebel and her evil behavior. He refused to listen to any of Jezebel's messengers. Jehu avoided her control and manipulation. He aggressively confronted the spirit behind the woman herself. Jehu finished what Elijah had begun, and we learn that God raised up a generation of people who would not bow to her or submit to her gods.

We have seen that the days of Elisha were the days of Jezebel, but there is one more part to add to it. They were also the days of Jehu, the relentless confrontational force that opposed the spirit of Jezebel. We have exposed what the spirit of Jezebel is, what she does, and how she does it. Once the spirit has been uncovered, it cannot be ignored, it must be dealt with. The Spirit of God that rested on Jehu dealt with Jezebel.

So a horseman went out to meet Jehu and said, "The king wants to know if you are coming in peace." Jehu replied, "What do you know about peace? Fall in behind me!" The watchman called out to the king, "The messenger has met them, but he's not returning." So the king sent out a second horseman. He rode up to them and said, "The king wants to know if you come in peace." Again Jehu answered, "What do you know about peace? Fall in behind me!" The watchman exclaimed, "The messenger has met them, but he isn't returning either! It must be Jehu son of Nimshi, for he's driving like a madman." (2 Kings 9:18-20, NLT)

Jehu had a warrior's disposition, drawn from a heart set on defeating evil in Israel. When dealing with Jezebel, it is likely you will have to put your reputation on the line. She is the master manipulator and her influence can be far-reaching through her messengers. Your personal integrity, character—everything—will be at stake when confronting Jezebel.

Everything on the Line

Not long after Paul began working for a ministry, he started noticing the symptoms of Jezebel at work in the church and leadership. The first major indicator was the lack of a pursuit of righteousness. Paul was viewed by staff members as being "religious" because he didn't drink alcohol and took a strong stance on sexual purity. Many of the male staff members were extremely effeminate, and others were overly concerned with their physical appearance. Everything he did seemed to be met with resistance. When Paul tried to talk to the senior pastor about it, he was confronted and rebuked severely by the other pastors. Paul was informed that he was the one that was "out of order," not the culture of the ministry, and he needed to "learn their DNA."

Over time, the resistance only grew worse. Paul was told repeatedly that he was "religious and needed to break free from the spirit of religion." Paul simply felt unwanted by the ministry and church staff, but he just couldn't figure out why. (You know when you're not wanted. You discern it by the Spirit.) Paul would not bend to their spiritual dispensation. He would not compromise his stance on purity and righteousness. Paul was very hesitant to do anything about all of this because he had recently dealt with a Jezebel spirit in his previous church, and he didn't want people to think he was a troublemaker. He just wanted to lay low.

Paul laid low for over a year, hoping that this spiritual opposition to him would go away. It didn't! It only got worse. He felt as if he was being forced out. Every staff member, at one time or another, had told him to his face, "We can't believe you're still here!" It finally got so bad that after months of prayer he started to ask God what he should do. Then he had a dream.

Paul wasn't much of a dreamer, and this dream was so vivid that after he awoke, it took him a moment to realize he had only been dreaming. In the dream, Paul and his wife had a massive confrontation with some pastors of the church staff and ultimately, they left the church. In the dream, Paul and his wife began to cry together, "No, Lord!" They didn't want to leave. Then all of a sudden, Paul was in another scene in the dream. He was in a very dimly lit room with many other people, all socializing. He sensed this was after a church service or something like that. He saw his senior pastor there, ran to him and began to whisper in his ear, telling him what had just happened between the other pastors and him.

After Paul finished recounting what had happened, his pastor pulled slowly away from him without saying a word. Paul sensed his pastor was siding with the other pastors. After the pastor pulled fully away, Paul noticed a very tall (6'5" or 6'6"), masculine woman, with a straight face, standing directly behind the pastor's left shoulder. Paul abruptly awoke. He knew immediately what the dream meant.

Paul told his wife first, then his mentor, and then the lead intercessor of his prayer team. All of them said the same thing: "Jezebel!" Now what? Paul prayed about it for a few days and finally felt the Lord leading him to go tell the pastor about his dream and what he discerned was going on in the church. Then the Lord clearly spoke to Paul about what he should do when he met with his senior pastor: "Wash your pastor's feet." Paul told his wife about the instructions God gave him. "Honey, are you sure?" she asked. "That's a little weird." *Paul agreed it was unusual. He had never washed anyone's feet before, aside from a specific church foot washing service. Paul assured his wife he had heard clearly what the Lord told him to do. She encouraged Paul to do what God told him to do.*

The next day, Paul set the appointment with his pastor, but he was nervous all day. He knew what was on the line—everything! Right before the meeting, he went to prayer again and laid pros-trate before the Lord. Paul asked God for His wisdom and assurance. Paul prayed, "Lord, I can lose everything, I could be fired...are you sure you want me to do this?" The Lord whispered to him, "Go...I've gone before you."

Paul went into the meeting and proceeded to tell the pastor everything. His voice cracked and his feet tapped, he was so nervous. He didn't want to be there. He didn't want to say these things. When he finished telling his pastor everything, Paul 's pastor shocked him by saying: "I'm aware of what you're talking about. I've seen these things too, but I don't throw people away. Would you be willing to sit down with all involved parties and talk this through?" Paul said he would. He was blown away at how receptive his pastor had been. He said: "Before I go, the Lord told me to wash your feet. May I?" His pastor said yes. So Paul got out the supplies and began to wash his pastor's feet, praying for him as he did so.

When Paul was finished, his pastor told him, "Hundreds of people have asked to wash my feet over the years. You are the only one I've ever allowed to do it. Paul felt humbled. He thanked his pastor and left his office.

Enter Jezebel! One hour later, Paul got a call from the pastor's assistant who was scheduling a meeting the next day for him and the other pastors. Paul asked the assistant if the senior pastor was going to be there and she told him he would not, that only the other staff pastors would be there. Paul called his pastor immediately. He could feel anxiety sucking his breath away. He asked his pastor why he wasn't going to be at the meeting. The pastor responded that the other staff pastors thought it would be better for them to meet with Paul alone. Paul told his pastor that he did not think a meeting without him was a good idea. His pastor then told Paul if he wanted him there, he would be there. Of course, Paul said he wanted him there.

Paul got another call from the pastor's assistant, and when asked, she said the senior pastor would not be attending. Paul told her he would not attend without the senior pastor there. Finally, a meeting was set...with Paul and the entire pastoral team. Paul walked into the room and the air was already thick with tension. Paul knew when he walked in that he was about to come face-to-face with his firing squad. The senior pastor opened by saying, "Paul, when you came to me and told me you thought Jezebel was working through them (pointing to the other pastors), you took this from a one to a ten by saying 'Jezebel.' If Jezebel was in operation, we would know. Now, tell them what you told me!" Paul couldn't believe his ears. His pastor had done a complete 180-degree turn. In private, he agreed with Paul and allowed him to wash his feet. Now, face-to-face with all the pastors, he wanted Paul to explain to the executive pastors how he believed the spirit of Jezebel was operating through them. Paul tried to be wise and humble in his wording, but the writing was on the wall.

The other pastors told Paul, "We think it's best if you move on." That was his last week at that church. Paul was asked to remove all his belongings within twenty-four hours.

That night, as he sat on the couch in his living room, Paul was emotionally broken. He had not wanted this to happen. He had not wanted a war. He had not wanted to confront Jezebel. He only wanted peace. Then the Lord spoke to him so very clearly, saying "Footwashing is preparation for betrayal!"

You put everything on the line when you confront Jezebel. But the truth is, without confronting Jezebel, there will never be authentic peace. You will lose everything!

"...WITHOUT CONFRONTING JEZEBEL, THERE WILL NEVER BE AUTHENTIC PEACE."

"Quick! Get my chariot ready!" King Joram commanded. Then King Joram of Israel and King Ahaziah of Judah rode out in their chariots to meet Jehu. They met him at the plot of land that had belonged to Naboth of Jezreel. King Joram demanded, "Do you come in peace, Jehu?" Jehu replied, "How can there be peace as long as the idolatry and witchcraft of your mother, Jezebel, are all around us?" Then King Joram turned the horses around and fled, shouting to King Ahaziah, "Treason, Ahaziah!" But Jehu drew his bow and shot Joram between the shoulders. The arrow pierced his heart, and he sank down dead in his chariot. (2 Kings 9:21-24, NLT)

Notice the king cried out, "Treason!" ("Treachery!" in other Bible versions). You will always be accused of being the ultimate betrayer when you confront Jezebel. You will be accused of being disloyal, betraying friendships, uncovering the family, hurting the church, devastating the congregation and even being demonically influenced. Remember, it's only treachery to the Jezebel spirit. To her captives, it is freedom!

This is the strategy for dealing with Jezebel. You war against the spirit, but lovingly confront the people through which the spirit is operating. In 1 Kings 19:15-17(NLT), we read: "Then the LORD told him, 'Go back the same way you came, and travel to the wilderness of Damascus. When you arrive there, anoint Hazael to be king of Aram.

"YOU WILL ALWAYS BE ACCUSED OF BEING THE ULTIMATE BETRAYER WHEN YOU CONFRONT JEZEBEL."

Then anoint Jehu grandson of Nimshi to be king of Israel, and anoint Elisha son of Shaphat from the town of Abel-meholah to replace you as my prophet. Anyone who escapes from Hazael will be killed by Jehu, and those who escape Jehu will be killed by Elisha!'" God told Elijah to, "Go back the same way you came." God was telling Elijah there was no way around Jezebel. She must be dealt with. And that's exactly what happened.

In 2 Kings 9:30-31, we read: "Then Jehu went to Jezreel. When Jezebel heard about it, she painted her eyes, arranged her hair and looked out of a window. As Jehu entered the gate, she asked, 'Have you come in peace, Zimri, you murderer of your master?'" Jezebel painted her eyes to create the appearance that would overawe Jehu and intimidate him. She painted her face because she was the goddess of war and she was ready for battle. She positioned herself atop the gate and struck a very public posture of complete defiance. Jehu was unimpressed. Second Kings 9:32-33 says: "He looked up at the window and called out, 'Who is on my side? Who?' Two or three eunuchs looked down at him. 'Throw her down!' Jehu said. So they threw her down, and some of her blood spattered the wall and the horses as they trampled her underfoot."

Consider that powerful phrase again, "Who is on the Lord's side?" Those who are on the side of the Lord will confront and war against the spirit of Jezebel. Her painted face was trampled into nothingness on the bottoms of the feet of righteousness. In Romans 16:20 (NLT), we read, "The God of peace will soon crush Satan under your feet. May the grace of our Lord Jesus be with you." Jezebel's painted face of fear, intimidation, manipulation, and domination was gone! *Let painted faces look in Jezebel's glass and see how they like themselves.* This picture is a reminder to all those who serve, cater to, or enable Jezebel: She will be cast down.

> Jehu went in and ate and drank. "Take care of that cursed woman," he said, "and bury her, for she was a king's daughter." But when they went out to bury her, they found nothing except her skull, her feet and her hands. They went back and told Jehu, who said, "This is the word of the LORD that he spoke through his servant Elijah the Tishbite: On the plot of ground at Jezreel dogs will devour Jezebel's flesh. Jezebel's body will be like refuse on the ground in the plot at Jezreel, so that no one will be able to say, 'This is Jezebel.'" (2 Kings 9:34-37)

Practical Ways of Dealing with Jezebel

The purpose of confronting Jezebel is for her to repent. Without godly sorrow, there can be no true repentance (2 Corinthians 7:10). Jezebel, the person, had many opportunities to repent, but she refused to do so. When we confront individuals who are influenced by the Jezebel spirit, we need to remember, it's not personal, it's spiritual!

The Church *must* return to the instruction that Jesus gave us on biblical confrontation. In Matthew 18:15-17 (NLT), we read: "If another believer sins against you, go privately and point out the offense. If the other person listens and confesses it, you have won that person back. But if you are unsuccessful, take one or two others with you and go back again, so that everything you say may be confirmed by two or three witnesses. If the person still refuses to listen, take your case to the church. Then if he or she won't accept the church's decision, treat that person as a pagan or a corrupt tax collector." If we follow Jesus's instructions on confrontation, it will more often than not prevent Jezebel from gaining power and influence in ministries. Often, we don't deal with the issues as they arise, so by the time we deal with them they have gotten completely out of control. If your church doesn't follow the teachings of Jesus, then find a church that does. If leaders will implement this biblical strategy, you will intercept many problems caused by the spirit of Jezebel before they arise. Those operating in the spirit of Jezebel will leave your ministry realizing your life and ministry are in order.

Once we are dead set on confronting the spirit of Jezebel, there are two primary strategies we must employ to defeat her: prayer and humility. Through prayer, we war in the heavenly places. In Matthew 18:18 (NLT), we read, "I tell you the truth, whatever you forbid on earth will be forbidden in heaven, and whatever you permit on earth will be permitted in heaven." Prayer will give you wisdom from above on the exact specifics in every situation.

Jezebel is fueled by her pride. You can't fight pride with pride. You can only fight pride with humility. Humility allows you to sidestep center stage and allows God to fight on your behalf. In Proverbs 15:33 (NLT), we read, "Fear of the LORD teaches wisdom; humility precedes honor." *Humility covers the gaps there may be in your spiritual armor.* Humility causes you to get so low that attacks pass right over your head. "Fear of the LORD teaches wisdom; humility precedes honor" (Proverbs 15:33, NLT).

"HUMILITY COVERS THE GAPS THERE MAY BE IN YOUR SPIRITUAL ARMOR."

Jesus was the greatest example of humility. He didn't respond to the attacks of Jezebel, *He allowed His Father to respond.* In John 19:8-10 (NLT), we read: "When Pilate heard this, he was more frightened than ever. He took Jesus back into the headquarters again and asked Him, 'Where are you from?' But Jesus gave no answer. 'Why don't you talk to me?' Pilate demanded. 'Don't you realize that I have the power to release you or crucify you?'" Wow, this is so powerful. Jesus never defended Himself. He was innocent, without sin, and He still wouldn't rebut false accusations against Him. Jesus allowed God the Father to vindicate Him (Isaiah 54:17). It's so imperative that when dealing with Jezebel, you refrain from defending yourself and justifying your behavior. That's what Jezebel does. It's your job to respond biblically and let God justify you. The lies about you may never cease. The lies and accusations against Jesus never stopped. To this day, they haven't stopped.

"JESUS WAS THE GREATEST EXAMPLE OF HUMILITY. HE DIDN'T RESPOND TO THE ATTACKS OF JEZEBEL, HE ALLOWED HIS FATHER TO RESPOND."

Hollywood movies have portrayed Jesus as having a sexual relationship with Mary Magdalene. News agencies and history TV channels air special reports and documentaries that attempt to debunk the real Jesus. In the face of this, it is important to remember that Jesus pressed through every lie, every accusation, and every assault from a place of humility in the shape of a cross. He laid down His life on the altar of humility with the power of all heaven. He was resurrected in mighty power. Through the power of Jesus, we can overcome all things. Through the power of Jesus, you will overcome the spirit of Jezebel! "They overcame him by the blood of the Lamb and by the word of their testimony" (Revelation 12:11, NIV).

Here are a few practical ways to deal with Jezebel...

1. Confront the Spirit

- Prayer and fasting loosens the spirit of Jezebel's grip and exposes her control and manipulation.
- If the Jezebel spirit is operating in you, it's your job to confront you.
- WARNING: Just because you confront her doesn't mean you will have peace!

2. Confront Individuals Being Controlled by the Spirit

- Follow the instructions in Matthew 18:15-17 on biblical confrontation. Do not divert from it.
- Don't resort to threats or any other Jezebel tactics. Be loving but firm in your rebuke. You don't need her approval.
- You fight pride with humility.
- Do not let her distract you with any emotional tactics, crying, outbursts, etc. (See her characteristics and behaviors, listed in Chapter 2.)

3. Take Authority Over All the Situations

- If the person operating in the spirit of Jezebel does not repent, you must remove them...or yourself.
- Don't wait for Jezebel to pull you aside and talk to you. You pull her aside and confront what needs to be confronted.
- Don't ask Jezebel to do anything for you. No side jobs, no favors, no projects.
- Don't receive Jezebel's curses. Plead the blood, declare you are blessed (as she cannot curse what God has blessed).

- Don't let Jezebel's words rest on you. Don't contemplate them.
- If you have been a victim of Jezebel and now see her spirit in you...repent!

Note to Pastors and Ministry Leaders

It's imperative that you teach your staff, team, friends, and family about the Jezebel spirit and her behaviors and characteristics. If you are not educated enough on the spirit, bring in someone to speak to your team who is. Teaching on this spirit will train your team how to be aware of it and detect it in its infancy stage. It will empower them to be the watchmen on the walls of your ministry they are called to be.

Many times, people wait way too long to confront those operating in the spirit of Jezebel, so she gains considerable influence and authority in ministries. When your team is instructed in recognizing and dealing with the Jezebel spirit, those who operate in it will stay away from your ministry or not stay for long.

Dealing With Jezebel: Do's and Don'ts

Do: Be humble and prayerful.

Don't: Don't use threats when confronting her. Calmly and firmly give her unmovable parameters.

CHAPTER 13

HEALING FROM JEZEBEL

A common misconception is, "Time heals all wounds." This is not true or biblical. If you broke your arm completely through the bone and just left it alone, it wouldn't matter how much time you allowed to go by, it would never again work to its full potential. There might be times when your arm doesn't hurt anymore, but you will never have full strength in it again. Your broken arm needs to be set and put back in place so it can heal correctly. Time alone doesn't heal all wounds; God heals all wounds.

Healing from Encounters with Jezebel

Encounters with Jezebel are extremely exhausting. They will drain you spiritually, mentally, and emotionally. You may need a period of time to recover, as you have encountered a demonic war. Demonic words and curses were spoken over your life. Detrimental soul ties were established. You need to spend time with the Holy Spirit and allow Him to begin to renew your mind. In Romans 12:2 (NIV), we read: "Do not conform any longer to the pattern of this world, but be transformed by the renewing of your mind. Then you will be able to test and approve what God's will is—his good, pleasing and perfect will." It's important for you to know, you are not cursed! Your life and ministry are not over! You are loved by God!

Some curses spoken over you can take deep roots within you. You need to begin to dig those up, rebuke them, and plead the blood of Jesus over them, one by one—*every single one*!

The Father's Blessing

In a weekday evening service, Austin ministered the Word. It seemed to be a regular service. Nothing in particular stood out to him. But as he closed his message, Austin heard the Lord tell him: "Have everyone in the church who wants the Father's blessing come up to the front of the church and form a single file line. Have the pastor come and lay hands on the people and bless them." Then the Lord said, "You stand in the front of the line and go first." Austin did exactly what the Lord told him to do as these kinds of unusual instructions had become normal to him. Austin obeyed the Lord and never thought about that night again.

About six months later, Austin and his pastor had a series of con-frontations. His pastor was very upset with him. In one particular conversation his pastor said to him, "You do not have my blessing." Shaking his head, he said, "You are not blessed!" The words pierced Austin's heart. His spiritual father and pastor had pronounced a curse over him—to his face. But the moment he said it, the Holy Spirit spoke clearly to him, saying, "You can't curse what you have already blessed." In that moment, the Holy Spirit had "kept" him.

God keeps His children. I imagine that if you looked back on your life's journey, you would recall times when God kept you, too. The truth is, God has been with you this entire time. In Hebrews 13:5-6 (NIV), we read: "God has said, 'Never will I leave you; never will I forsake you.' So we say with confidence, 'The Lord is my helper; I will not be afraid. What can man do to me?'" His presence is heal-ing; His Word (the Bible) is healing. Most of all, His still, small voice is healing!

Healing from Confronting Jezebel

When Jezebel is confronted, she becomes the goddess of war. When she is in war mode she can do some major damage. She damages hearts, minds, reputations, relationships—nothing is off limits. The greatest thing she damages is your future.

Jezebel Plans for the Future

Brian was an energetic young minister. He and his wife, Katie, were fresh out of Bible college and Brian was ready to take on the world. In ministry, he excelled quickly, just as he had done at everything else in life. As a former military officer, he was disciplined in creating infrastructure and a well thought-out "plan of attack." He combined both his military training and Bible college training to implement a powerful war strategy for taking on the gates of hell. Brian's ministry exploded! In the first few years of ministry, his youth church surpassed over 500 teenagers. Brian moved heavily in the prophetic and other spiritual gifts, and he began to see a true revival break out in his city.

In one service, God radically touched the captain of the football team. Brian gave him a prophetic word and he ended up giving his life to the Lord and inviting the entire football team to church. Drug dealers, homosexuals, and gang members were all getting saved and coming to Jesus. Just as in many true moves of the Spirit, Jezebel was drawn to them and began to operate amongst them. Brian had a female assistant who served him faithfully. She was a pretty girl who came up through the ranks of the ministry, but she had a very seductive, flirtatious way about her. It was a spirit!

At some point, she began to mimic Brian's wife, Katie. She styled her hair to be like Katie's, dressed like her, and even began to imitate some of her mannerisms. It was just...weird, as if she was trying to become Katie. But Katie had one thing the assistant couldn't mimic— she had Brian. Unfortunately, Brian was next on the assistant's wish list. She really poured it on, flirting heavily and becoming very touchy-feely around him. It was clear she was trying to tempt Brian sexually.

Brian was a man of God with integrity. He knew he was being tempted and that it was wrong. He began to set up boundaries except for one thing—he allowed her to stay close to the family. This assistant did everything for them, from grocery shopping to picking up their kids from school. It was as if she was an actual part of the family.

Meanwhile, Katie began developing an increasingly painful, chronic illness. She visited the doctor many times but they could not pinpoint the cause of it. Her illness grew worse and worse and remained undiagnosed.

Years went by, new ministries were begun, families were raised together and the relationships remained the same. Little did they know, the spirit of Jezebel hibernated within this family and ministry, undetected for years! About five years later, Brian, Katie, the assistant, and their ministry team moved across the country to start a church of their own. Brian and Katie sold everything they owned and moved to the city in which God had called them to start a church. The church was birthed and soon exploded, growing to over 500 members in the first year. God was moving...and Jezebel was about to come out of hibernation.

Brian and Katie began to notice problems with staff members. People began acting out and they were getting uncharacteristic resistance from their core leadership team. A few troublemakers popped up in the church. They noticed that all of these ladies seemed to be drawn to Brian's assistant, who by that time carried significant influence within the ministry. Thank God, He sent a little old lady, an intercessor, to become part of Brian and Katie's church.

One day, this precious lady asked Brian if he was aware of the spirit of Jezebel...because she was aware of him. A light bulb went on in Brian's spirit. Everything started coming together, like a dark, dramatic movie thriller. All the pieces started coming together. He describes it here in his own words:

> *The sickness was parallel with the Jezebel spirit, even down to the exact time frame of when the spirit began to make its moves. The spirit came in subtly, making small advances, hiding in secrecy until it could take root, laying traps for both the present and future. One instance only compounded*

another, as if it was morphing and adapting, yet determined to advance. Before we knew it, Jezebel had fully infiltrated our lives and become a semi-permanent fixture, making herself almost non-removable. This is exactly the path Katie's sickness took as well. The crazy thing is, we never recognized it fully until years later because we were uneducated about this spirit and its operation.

Brian and Katie prayed for wisdom and acted quickly. They brought order back to their lives, family, and ministry. Brian took spiritual authority over his ministry and family. His assistant and her family left the church a few months later. Brian and Katie's church still continues to grow and the Spirit of God is thriving there.

Brian wanted me to share with you one big thing he learned from his encounter with the Jezebel spirit: Jezebel doesn't infiltrate your life and ministry to destroy where you are, but where you are going! This spirit might not even begin to fully manifest itself until you begin your final work. Don't let your past keep you from your future. Your future must be more important than your past. Many people won't let go of the past, choosing to linger there, missing out on what God holds for them now and in the future. Forgiveness forces us to let go of our past and lay hold of our future. Remember Isaiah 43:18 (NIV): "Forget the former things; do not dwell on the past."

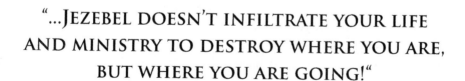

"...JEZEBEL DOESN'T INFILTRATE YOUR LIFE AND MINISTRY TO DESTROY WHERE YOU ARE, BUT WHERE YOU ARE GOING!"

Healing from Becoming Jezebel

You may be reading this book and thinking to yourself, *Oh my good-ness, I think I have become a Jezebel.* Perhaps as you've read this book you have seen many of the characteristics of Jezebel in your life. If that's true, I'm so glad you are reading this because you are no lon-ger self-deceived and now know how to break the spirit of Jezebel off your life. You can begin to heal and help others heal. It may even be that you have hurt people and need to begin to heal from that also.

In the Bible, we see that David knew what it felt like to begin to become what he despised. Remember, Saul walked in the Jezebel spirit and that spirit had her eyes fixed on David—she was after him. David was a worshiper who had a pure heart before God and Saul could not be more jealous of him. Saul tenaciously pursued David and viciously attempted to kill him.

> This was their song: "Saul has killed his thousands, and David his ten thousands!" This made Saul very angry. "What's this?" he said. "They credit David with ten thousands and me with only thousands. Next they'll be making him their king!" So from that time on Saul kept a jealous eye on David. The very next day a tormenting spirit* from God overwhelmed Saul, and he began to rave in his house like a madman. David was playing the harp, as he did each day. But Saul had a spear in his hand, and he suddenly hurled it at David, intending to pin him to the wall. But David escaped him twice. (1 Samuel 18:7-11, NLT)

David had to dodge Saul's spears to stay alive. He never once threw a spear back at Saul. David knew that if he threw a spear back, the moment it left his hand he would be fighting like Saul or Jeze-bel—he would become like them. The spear belonged to Saul. It was not David's spear to throw. David had already turned down Saul's armor and weaponry the first time, so why would he use it now? In 1 Samuel 17:38-39 (NIV), we read: "Then Saul dressed David in his own tunic. He put a coat of armor on him and a bronze helmet on his head. David fastened on his sword over the tunic and tried walking around, because he was not used to them. 'I cannot go in these,' he said to Saul, 'because I am not used to them.' So he took them off." David fought under the anointing of the Spirit of God. If he threw Saul's spear back at him, he would be fighting in the *flesh* of Saul or the *flesh* of Jezebel. I believe this is why David refused to kill Saul in a cave in this account from 1 Samuel 24:4-6: "The men said, 'This is the day the Lord spoke of when he said to you, "I will give your enemy into your hands for you to deal with as you wish."' Then David crept up unnoticed and cut off a corner of Saul's robe. Afterward, David was conscience-stricken for having cut off a corner of his robe. He said to his men, 'The Lord forbid that I should do such a thing to my master, the Lord's anointed, or lift my hand against him; for he is the anointed of the Lord.'"

For years, I never understood why David referred to Saul as the Lord's anointed. After all, he wasn't, but David was! In 1 Samuel 16:13 (NIV), we read: "So Samuel took the horn of oil and anointed him in the presence of his brothers, and from that day on the Spirit of the LORD came upon David in power. Samuel then went to Ramah." I believe David wasn't talking about Saul. I believe he was talking about himself. I believe he was saying, "If I touch Saul, I change myself!"

Saul threw spears, the Pharisees threw rocks, and Jezebel throws words. You heal from becoming Jezebel by repenting and no longer fighting like Jezebel. Don't fight in her pride. Don't use her

"SAUL THREW SPEARS, THE PHARISEES THREW ROCKS, AND JEZEBEL THROWS WORDS."

manipulation tactics. Don't operate in a controlling spirit. Don't threaten her. Don't "need" to be right all the time. Fight with love, prayer, grace, humility, and forgiveness! Refuse Saul's armor and put on God's!

> Therefore put on the full armor of God, so that when the day of evil comes, you may be able to stand your ground, and after you have done everything, to stand. Stand firm then, with the belt of truth buckled around your waist, with the breastplate of righteousness in place, and with your feet fitted with the readiness that comes from the gospel of peace. In addition to all this, take up the shield of faith, with which you can extinguish all the flaming arrows of the evil one. Take the helmet of salvation and the sword of the Spirit, which is the word of God. And pray in the Spirit on all occasions with all kinds of prayers and requests. With this in mind, be alert and always keep on praying for all the saints. (Ephesians 6:13-18, NIV)

Like David, we are called to fight, empowered by the Spirit of God, under the anointing of the Holy Spirit, not in our flesh.

It's Time for Deliverance

Deliverance is when you are truly, totally set free. You're not out on probation...you are free to go. You are free to get moving toward your future. Only Jesus can bring true deliverance, as He declared in Luke 4:18-19 (NIV): "The Spirit of the Lord is on me, because he has anointed me to preach good news to the poor. He has sent me to proclaim freedom for the prisoners and recovery of sight for the blind, to release the oppressed, to proclaim the year of the Lord's favor." Healing can be a process, but healing begins when deliverance is set in motion. Mine came from meeting John Paul Jackson.

My Story

*I was in Austin, Texas, ministering for one of my best friends. About that time, I come across the book, **Needless Casualties of War**, by John Paul Jackson. I didn't know John Paul, but I had heard of him. As I read his book, the wisdom on its pages had a great impact on my prayer life and spiritual warfare. I was halfway through the book when I heard the Holy Spirit say, "You need him in your life to fulfill your life's assignment." That was it.*

When I got back home, I called his office. I told his assistant, "I'm not a weirdo! I know you guys get a thousand calls a week of people wanting to talk to John Paul, but I felt the Lord tell me to call. This is a little weird and awkward because I don't want anything, I don't need anything, I just want to introduce myself to John Paul." His assistant, who is both wise and discerning, said, "I really feel God in this call. I will set up an appointment."

A few months later, Heather and I ended up meeting with John Paul and his team in Dallas. We sat down and I just began to share my heart. I told him every detail I possibly could. I wanted to be completely transparent. When I was done sharing, a few hours had gone by. I had no idea how he would respond, but he looked at us gently and said, "The Lord spoke to me before you got here and told me to stand with you, and bless you." Then he prayed a simple prayer for us; it wasn't long. When he had finished, I felt a change in me. It was as if a giant ball had slowly begun to roll. I felt my process of deep healing begin to roll forward. I felt a spirit of deliverance being released within me.

I've had many great friends who have loved me, encouraged me, and spoken life over me, but as John Paul prayed, I felt my deliverance was set in motion.

I believe God wants to set your complete healing and deliverance in motion today! God wants to heal you and set you free from the pain of encountering Jezebel, confronting her, or becoming her. As I stated previously, I want to encourage you to submit yourself to godly, Spirit-led, humble leaders who can pray with you and walk you through this process. Do not become rebellious and unsubmissive, like Jezebel. I want to encourage you *not* to receive Jezebel's curses over your life. Today (right now), bind them, rebuke them, and plead the blood of Jesus over your life. Boldly declare over yourself the truth that you are blessed! Remember Numbers 23:20 (NIV): "I have received a command to bless; he has blessed, and I cannot change it."

The weight of battling Jezebel can be overwhelming, but even surviving her warfare creates the humility you need to defeat her.

"THE WEIGHT OF BATTLING JEZEBEL CAN BE OVERWHELMING, BUT EVEN SURVIVING HER WARFARE CREATES THE HUMILITY YOU NEED TO DEFEAT HER."

Final Story

I was in a powerful service with Lou Engel as he ministered on breaking the spirit of Jezebel over regions. He told the story of a 40-day fast the Lord led him into to defeat the spirit of Jezebel over his life. As the service continued, I began to feel waves of the power of God hit me. I began to convulse slowly and shake under the power of God. (This had never happened to me before.) I began to lean forward slowly, bending beneath the weight of God's glory, as waves of His presence washed over me. I ended up hunched over completely, to the point where my head was only a foot off the ground. I was still standing, but I was completely bowed over. In that position, the Lord spoke to me. He said, "The weight of facing Jezebel has brought you to this place. But your knee hasn't bent to her. She has caused you to bow before me!"

Elijah was in a similar spiritual state. He felt the weight of battling with Jezebel. As he felt this weight, God spoke to him something similar in 1 Kings 19:18 (NLT): "Yet I will preserve 7,000 others in Israel who have never bowed down to Baal or kissed him!" God is raising up a generation of prophets and priests to war against Jezebel; young people who refuse to bow in submission to her or kiss her lips of seduction. You are not the only one!

Don't let Jezebel's words rest on you and take root in your heart. Don't repeat one more word she has said, nor contemplate her words for even one more second. Dream about your future because Jezebel has failed to destroy it. You are blessed and highly favored. God is going to use your life for His glory!

Pray this prayer of faith out loud:

Jesus, I love you, and I know you love me. Right now, I release your presence into this place. This is your place, God. Jesus, you have all authority and in your name, I have access to that authority. So right now, I bind and rebuke every word that Jezebel has spoken over me. (List them.) I REFUSE ALL OF THEM! I declare no spirit but the Holy Spirit has authority in my life. I submit to the Holy Spirit. I declare your lordship in my life, King Jesus. Father, your Word says that Jesus intercedes for me. So Jesus, I ask you to pray over me right now. In JESUS'S NAME, I rebuke the spirit of Jezebel—I rebuke your witchcraft. I rebuke the effects of witchcraft and I command peace in my heart in JESUS'S name. I forgive those who have come against me and I release them to you, God. Lord, I ask you to forgive me for how I've handled this in the wrong way, in areas. In the name of Jesus Christ, I rebuke the spirit of Jezebel in, on, and around me! Father, help me to be submissive, humble, and pure-hearted before you. I love you, Jesus! I love you, Jesus! I love you, Jesus! (Feel free to repeat this as many times as you want!)

Author's Note

Let me leave you with an encouragement. If you have continually prayed this prayer or a prayer like this, yet have not seen a change, get people to partner with you in this. I suggest individuals who are at a higher level of spiritual authority. The Bible teaches us the power when believers unify.

A person standing alone can be attacked and defeated, but two can stand back-to-back and conquer. Three are even better, for a triple-braided cord is not easily broken. (Ecclesiastes 4:12, NLT)

How good and pleasant it is when brothers live together in unity! (Psalm 133:1, NIV)

Finally, begin the process of complete healing by entering a true deliverance process. Find a Spirit-filled church that practices biblical deliverance through individual ministry, mentorship, discipleship, or counseling and begin the process of renewal.

Do not conform any longer to the pattern of this world, but be transformed by the renewing of your mind. Then you will be able to test and approve what God's will is—his good, pleasing and perfect will. (Romans 12:2, NIV)

Dealing With Jezebel: Do's and Don'ts

Do: When people curse you, bless them in return.

Don't: Don't receive her curses or what might sound like blessings.

DEALING WITH JEZEBEL
DO'S AND DON'TS
(QUICK REFERENCE)

Chapter 1: Who Was Jezebel?
Do: Always listen to your God-given discernment and wisdom.
Don't: Don't compromise with Jezebel.

Chapter 2: Recognizing Jezebel's Characteristics and Behaviors
Do: Always have someone with you when you meet with or confront Jezebel. Under no circumstance are you to meet with her alone.
Don't: Don't accept any gifts or personal favors from Jezebel.

Chapter 3: Jezebel's Weapons of War
Do: Always stand up for righteousness, integrity, and purity, no matter who comes against you.
Don't: Don't let Jezebel misuse or misquote Scripture to you or about you.

Chapter 4: Effects of Witchcraft
Do: Allow God's voice (the Word) to rebuke Jezebel's voice.
Don't: Don't let Jezebel lay hands on you or pray for you. Ever!

Chapter 5: Jezebel and Self-Deception
Do: On a regular basis, ask God to search your heart for things you have hidden from Him and yourself.
Don't: Don't assume that since you've grown spiritually, you are immune to falling prey to self-deception (Jezebel spirit).

Chapter 6: The Spirit of Jezebel
Do: Confront the person but spiritually war against the spirit of Jezebel.
Don't: Don't allow any single person to take your focus off the spirit of Jezebel that is in operation.

Chapter 7: The Family Tree
Do: Admit to your family, children, and friends when you are wrong. Imitate the humility of Jesus.
Don't: Don't allow Jezebel around your children or to be divisive in your marriage.

Chapter 8: Spiritual Abortion
Do: Find a righteous man or woman of God who wants to be a spiritual father or mother. Learn from him or her.
Don't: Don't become bitter and give up on biblical discipleship, mentorship, and sonship.

Chapter 9: The Sensual Side of Jezebel
Do: Live a life with a high standard of righteousness and integrity. Tell others of these standards to keep you accountable to them.
Don't: Don't hide your own sexual temptations and sin. Confess them. This will protect you from being seduced into sexual sin by Jezebel.

Chapter 10: Jezebel Has Friends (Familiar Spirits)
Do: Do not believe everything people say about others; make sure you are not allowing faultfinder to deceive you.
Don't: Don't accept any favors or gifts from Jezebel. Don't accept anything that would cause you to owe her any favors or be indebted to her.

Chapter 11: Kill the Messenger
Do: Rebuke every lie spoken to you and over you, every time you hear one.
Don't: Don't give in to the need to tell other people what Jezebel has said about you or over you.

Chapter 12: Dealing with and Defeating Jezebel

Do: Be humble and prayerful.

Don't: Don't use threats when confronting her. Calmly and firmly give her unmovable parameters.

Chapter 13: Healing from Jezebel

Do: When people curse you, bless them in return.

Don't: Don't receive her curses or what might sound like blessings.

Notes

1 http://www.xxxchurch.com/extras/stats.html

2 http://www.adaa.org/about-adaa/press-room/facts-statistics

3 http://en.wikipedia.org/wiki/Shooting_the_messenger

About the Author

Landon Schott is the founder and president of REVtv.com, a 24/7 online youth and young adult network dedicated to turning the heart of a generation to Jesus through Christ-centered media. He is also the president of FaithChannel.com, a digital media faith-based network.

Landon and his wife, Heather, founded The Rev Ministries in 2008, a media ministry that airs TV programs internationally. Landon and Heather travel around the nation as a prophetic voice, ministering at churches, conferences, and crusades to all generations.

Landon and Heather have one daughter, Payton Olivia Lynn. They plan on growing their own family as they work hard to grow God's family. Their mission in life is simple: To make Jesus famous!

Follow Landon and Heather on Twitter & Facebook:
Twitter: @landonschott
Facebook: Facebook.com/landonschott
Twitter: @heather_schott
Facebook: Facebook.com/heatherlynnschott

For booking or more information, go to:
info@therev.com
TheRev.com
REVtv.com

CPSIA information can be obtained at www.ICGtesting.com
Printed in the USA
BVOW11s2105130815

412998BV00008B/157/P